Henry Harland

Gray Roses

Henry Harland

Gray Roses

ISBN/EAN: 9783744685986

Printed in Europe, USA, Canada, Australia, Japan

Cover: Foto ©Thomas Meinert / pixelio.de

More available books at **www.hansebooks.com**

GRAY ROSES

BY HENRY HARLAND

BOSTON: ROBERTS BROS., 1895

LONDON: JOHN LANE, VIGO ST

CONTENTS.

	PAGE
THE BOHEMIAN GIRL	9
MERCEDES	49
A BROKEN LOOKING-GLASS	61
THE REWARD OF VIRTUE	71
A RE-INCARNATION	87
FLOWER O' THE QUINCE	109
WHEN I AM KING	121
A RESPONSIBILITY	141
CASTLES NEAR SPAIN	159

THE BOHEMIAN GIRL.

THE BOHEMIAN GIRL.

I

I WOKE up very gradually this morning, and it took me a little while to bethink myself where I had slept, — that it had not been in my own room in the Cromwell Road. I lay a-bed, with eyes half-closed, drowsily looking forward to the usual procession of sober-hued London hours, and, for the moment, quite forgot the journey of yesterday, and how it had left me in Paris, a guest in the smart new house of my old friend, Nina Childe. Indeed, it was not until somebody tapped on my door, and I roused myself to call out "Come in," that I noticed the strangeness of the wall-paper, and then, after an instant of perplexity, suddenly remembered. Oh, with a wonderful lightening of the spirit, I can tell you.

A white-capped, brisk young woman, with a fresh-colored, wholesome peasant face, came in, bearing a tray, — Jeanne, Nina's femme-de-chambre.

"Bonjour, monsieur," she cried cheerily. "I bring monsieur his coffee." And her announcement was followed by a fragrance, — the softly-sung response of the coffee-sprite. Her tray, with its pretty freight of silver and linen, primrose butter, and gently browned pain-de-gruau, she set down on the table at my elbow;

then she crossed the room and drew back the window-curtains, making the rings tinkle crisply on the metal rods, and letting in a gush of dazzling sunshine. From where I lay I could see the house-fronts opposite glow pearly gray in shadow, and the crest of the slate roofs sharply print itself on the sky, like a black line on a sheet of scintillant blue velvet. Yet, a few minutes ago, I had been fancying myself in the Cromwell Road.

Jeanne, gathering up my scattered garments, to take them off and brush them, inquired, by the way, if monsieur had passed a comfortable night.

"As the chambermaid makes your bed, so must you lie in it," I answered. "And you know whether my bed was smoothly made."

Jeanne smiled indulgently. But her next remark — did it imply that she found me rusty? "Here's a long time that you have n't been in Paris."

"Yes," I admitted; "not since May, and now we're in November."

"We have changed things a little, have we not?" she demanded, with a gesture that left the room, and included the house, the street, the quarter.

"In effect," assented I.

"Monsieur desires his hot water?" she asked, abruptly irrelevant.

But I could be, or at least seem, abruptly irrelevant too. "Mademoiselle — is she up?"

"Ah, yes, monsieur. Mademoiselle has been up since eight. She awaits you in the salon. La voilà qui joue," she added, pointing to the floor.

Nina had begun to play scales in the room below.

"Then you may bring me my hot water," I said.

II

The scales continued while I was dressing, and many desultory reminiscences of the player, and vague reflections upon the unlikelihood of her adventures, went flitting through my mind to their rhythm. Here she was, scarcely turned thirty, beautiful, brilliant, rich in her own right, as free in all respects to follow her own will as any man could be, with Camille happily at her side, a well-grown, rosy, merry miss of twelve, — here was Nina, thus, to-day; and yet, a mere little ten years ago, I remembered her . . . ah, in a very different plight indeed. True, she has got no more than her deserts; she has paid for her success, every pennyweight of it, in hard work and self-denial. But one is so expectant, here below, to see Fortune capricious, that, when for once in a way she bestows her favors where they are merited, one can't help feeling rather dazed. One is so inured to seeing honest Effort turn empty-handed from her door.

Ten little years ago — but no. I must begin further back. I must tell you something about Nina's father.

III

He was an Englishman who lived for the greater part of his life in Paris. I would say he was a painter, if he had not been equally a sculptor, a musician, an architect, a writer of verse, and a university coach. A doer of so many things is inevitably suspect; you will imagine that he must have bungled them all.

On the contrary, whatever he did, he did with a considerable degree of accomplishment. The landscapes he painted were very fresh and pleasing, delicately colored, with lots of air in them, and a dreamy, suggestive sentiment. His brother sculptors declared that his statuettes were modelled with exceeding dash and directness; they were certainly fanciful and amusing. I remember one that I used to like immensely,—Titania driving to a tryst with Bottom, her chariot a lily, daisies for wheels, and for steeds a pair of mettlesome field-mice. I doubt if he ever got a commission for a complete house; but the staircases he designed, the fire-places, and other bits of buildings, everybody thought original and graceful. The tunes he wrote were lively and catching, the words never stupid, sometimes even strikingly happy, epigrammatic; and he sang them delightfully, in a robust, hearty baritone. He coached the youth of France, for their examinations, in Latin and Greek, in history, mathematics, general literature,—in goodness knows what not; and his pupils failed so rarely that, when one did, the circumstance became a nine days' wonder. The world beyond the Students' Quarter had never heard of him, but there he was a celebrity and a favorite; and, strangely enough for a man with so many strings to his bow, he contrived to pick up a sufficient living.

He was a splendid creature to look at, tall, stalwart, full-blooded, with a ruddy open-air complexion; a fine bold brow and nose; brown eyes, humorous, intelligent, kindly, that always brightened flatteringly when they met you; and a vast quantity of bluish-gray hair and beard. In his dress he affected (very wisely, for they became him excellently) velvet jackets, flannel shirts, loosely knotted ties, and wide-brimmed soft-felt hats. Marching down the Boulevard St. Michel, his broad shoulders well thrown back, his head erect, chin high in air, his whole person radiating health, power, contentment, and the pride of them, he was a sight worth seeing, spirited, picturesque, prepossessing. You could not have passed him without noticing him; without wondering who he was, confident he was somebody; without admiring him, and feeling that there went a man it would be interesting to know.

He was, indeed, charming to know; he was the hero, the idol, of a little sect of worshippers, young fellows who loved nothing better than to sit at his feet. On the Rive Gauche, to be sure, we are, for the most part, birds of passage; a student arrives, tarries a little, then departs. So, with the exits and entrances of seniors and nouveaux, the personnel of old Childe's following varied from season to season; but numerically it remained pretty much the same. He had a studio, with a few living-rooms attached, somewhere up in the fastnesses of Montparnasse, though it was seldom thither that one went to seek him. He received at his café, the Café Bleu,— the Café Bleu, which has since blown into the monster café of the Quarter, the noisiest, the rowdiest, the most flamboyant. But I am writing (alas!) of twelve, thirteen, fifteen years ago; in those days the Café Bleu consisted of a single oblong room, — with a sanded floor, a dozen tables, and two waiters, Eugène and Hippolyte, — where Madame Chanve, the patronne, in lofty insulation behind her counter, reigned, if you please, but where Childe, her principal client, governed. The bottom of the shop, at any rate, was reserved exclusively to his use. There he dined, wrote his letters, dispensed his hospitalities; he had his own piano there, if you can believe me, his foils and boxing-gloves; from the absinthe hour till bed-time there was his habitat, his den. And woe to the passing stranger who, mistaking the Café Bleu for an ordinary house of call, ventured, during that consecrated period, to drop in. Nothing would be said, nothing done; we would not even trouble to stare at the intruder. Yet he would seldom stop to finish his consommation, or he would bolt it. He would feel something in the air; he would know he was out of place. He would fidget a little, frown a little, and get up meekly, and slink into the street. Human magnetism is such a subtle force. And Madame Chanve did n't mind in the least; she preferred a bird in the hand to a brace in the bush. From half a dozen to a score of us dined at her long table every evening; as many more drank her appetizers in the afternoon and came again at night for grog or coffee. You see, it was a sort of club, a club of which Childe was at once the chairman and the object. If we had had a written constitution, it must have begun: "The purpose of this association is the enjoyment of the society of Alfred Childe."

Ah, those afternoons, those dinners, those ambrosial nights! If the weather was kind, of course we would begin our session on the terrasse, sipping our vermouth, puffing our cigarettes, laughing our laughs, tossing hither and thither our light ball of gossip, vaguely conscious of the perpetual ebb and flow and murmur of people in the Boulevard, while the setting sun turned Paris to a marvellous water-color, all pale lucent tints, amber and alabaster and mother-of-pearl, with amethystine shadows. Then, one by one, those of us who were dining elsewhere would slip away; and at a sign from Hippolyte the others would move indoors, and take their places down either side of the long narrow table, Childe at the head, his daughter Nina next him. And presently with what a clatter of knives and forks, clinking of glasses, and babble of human voices the Café Bleu would echo. Madame Chanve's kitchen was not a thing to boast of, and her price, for the Latin Quarter, was rather high, — I think we paid three francs, wine included, which would be for most of us distinctly a prix-de-luxe. But oh, it was such fun; we were so young; Childe was so delightful! The fun was best, of course, when we were few, and could all sit up near to him, and none need lose a word. When we were many there would be something like a scramble for good seats.

I ask myself whether, if I could hear him again to-day, I should think his talk as wondrous as I thought it then. Then I could thrill at the verse of Musset, and linger lovingly over the prose of Théophile; I could laugh at the wit of Gustave Droz, and weep at the pathos . . . it costs me a pang to own it, but yes, I'm afraid . . . I could weep at the pathos of Henry Murger; and these have all suffered such a sad sea-change since. So I could sit, hour after hour, in a sort of ecstasy, listening to the talk of Nina's father. It flowed from him like wine from a full measure, easily, smoothly, abundantly. He had a ripe, genial voice, and an enunciation that made crystals of his words; whilst his range of subjects was as wide as the earth and the sky. He would talk to you of God and man, of metaphysics, ethics, the last new play, murder, or change of ministry; of books, of pictures, specifically, or of the general principles of literature and painting; of people, of sunsets, of Italy, of the high seas, of the Paris streets — of what, in fine, you pleased. Or he would spin you yarns, sober, farcical, veridical, or invented. And, with transitions infinitely rapid, he would be serious, jocose — solemn, ribald — earnest, flippant — logical, whimsical, turn and turn about. And in every sentence, in its form or in its substance, he would wrap a surprise for you, — it was the unexpected word, the unexpected assertion, sentiment, conclusion, that constantly arrived. Meanwhile it would enhance your enjoyment mightily to watch his physiognomy, the movements of his great gray, shaggy head, the lightening and darkening of his eyes, his smile, his frown, his occasional slight shrug or gesture. But the oddest thing was this, that he could take as well as give; he could listen, — surely a rare talent in a monologist. Indeed, I have never known a man who could make *you* feel so interesting.

After dinner he would light an immense brown meerschaum pipe, and smoke for a quarter-hour or so in silence; then he would play a game or two of chess with some one; and by and by he would open his piano, and sing to us till midnight.

IV

I speak of him as old, and indeed we always called him Old Childe among ourselves; yet he was barely fifty. Nina, when I first made her acquaintance, must have been a girl of sixteen or seventeen; though — tall, with an amply rounded, mature-seeming figure — if one had judged from her appearance, one would have fancied her three or four years older. For that matter, she looked then very much as she looks now; I can perceive scarcely any alteration. She had the same dark hair, gathered up in a big smooth knot behind, and breaking into a tumult of little ringlets over her forehead; the same clear, sensitive complexion; the same rather large, full-lipped mouth, tip-tilted nose, soft chin, and merry mischievous eyes. She moved in the same way, with the same leisurely, almost lazy grace, that could, however, on occasions, quicken to an alert, elastic vivacity; she had the same voice, a trifle deeper than most women's, and of a quality never so delicately nasal, which made it racy and characteristic; the same fresh ready laughter. There was something arch, something a little sceptical, a little quizzical in her expression, as if, perhaps, she were disposed to take the world, more or less, with a grain of salt; at the same time there was something rich, warm-blooded, luxurious, suggesting that she would know how to savor its pleasantnesses with complete enjoyment. But if you felt that she was by way of being the least bit satirical in her view of things, you felt too that she was altogether good-natured, and even that, at need, she could show herself spontaneously kind, generous, devoted. And if you inferred that her temperament inclined rather towards the sensuous than the ascetic, believe me, it did not lessen her attractiveness.

At the time of which I am writing now, the sentiment that reigned between Nina and Old Childe's retinue of young men was chiefly an esprit-de-corps. Later on, we all fell in love with her; but for the present we were simply amiably fraternal. We were united to her by a common enthusiasm; we were fellow-celebrants at her ancestral altar, — or, rather, she was the high priestess there, we were her acolytes. For, with her, filial piety did in very truth partake of the nature of religion; she really, literally, idolized her father. One only needed to watch her for three minutes, as she sat beside him, to understand the depth and ardor of her emotion: how she adored him, how she admired him and believed in him, how proud of him she was, how she rejoiced in him. "Oh, you think you know my father," I remember her saying to us once. "Nobody knows him. Nobody is great enough to know him. If people knew him, they would fall down and kiss the ground he walks on." It is certain she deemed him the wisest, the noblest, the handsomest, the most gifted, of human kind. That little gleam of mockery in her eye died out instantly when she looked at him, when she spoke of him or listened to him; instead, there came a tender light of love, and her face grew pale with the fervor of her affection. Yet, when he jested, no one laughed more promptly or more heartily than she. In those days I was perpetually trying to write fiction; and Old Childe was my inveterate hero. I forget in how many ineffectual manuscripts, under what various dread disguises, he was afterwards reduced to ashes; I am afraid, in one case, a scandalous distortion of him got abroad in print. Publishers are sometimes ill-advised; and thus the indiscretions of

our youth may become the confusions of our age.
The thing was in three volumes, and called itself a
novel; and of course the fatuous author had to make
a bad business worse by presenting a copy to his
victim. I shall never forget the look Nina gave me
when I asked her if she had read it; I grow hot even
now as I recall it. I had waited and waited expecting
her compliments; and at last I could wait no longer,
and so asked her; and she answered me with a look!
It was weeks, I am not sure it was n't months, before
she took me back to her good graces. But Old Childe
was magnanimous; he sent me a little pencil-drawing
of his head, inscribed in the corner, "To Frankenstein,
from his Monster."

V

It was a queer life for a girl to live; that happy-go-
lucky life of the Latin Quarter, lawless and unpremed-
itated, with a café for her school-room, and none but
men for comrades; but Nina liked it, and her father
had a theory in his madness. He was a Bohemian,
not in practice only, but in principle; he preached
Bohemianism as the most rational manner of existence, maintaining that it developed what was in-
trinsic and authentic in one's character, saved one
from the artificial, and brought one into immediate
contact with the realities of the world; and he protested he could see no reason why a human being
should be "cloistered and contracted" because of her
sex. "What would not hurt my son, if I had one,
will not hurt my daughter. It will make a man of

her — without making her the less a woman." So he took her with him to the Café Bleu, and talked in her presence quite as freely as he might have talked had she been absent. As, in the greater number of his theological, political, and social convictions, he was exceedingly unorthodox, she heard a good deal, no doubt, that most of us would scarcely consider edifying for our daughters' ears; but he had his system, he knew what he was about. "The question whether you can touch pitch and remain undefiled," he said, "depends altogether upon the spirit in which you approach it. The realities of the world, the realities of life, the real things of God's universe, — what have we eyes for, if not to envisage them? Do so fearlessly, honestly, with a clean heart, and, man or woman, you can only be the better for it." Perhaps his system was a shade too simple, a shade too obvious, for this complicated planet; but he held to it in all sincerity. It was in pursuance of the same system, I dare say, that he taught Nina to fence, and to read Latin and Greek, as well as to play the piano, and turn an omelette. She could ply a foil against the best of us.

And then, quite suddenly, he died.

I think it was in March or April; anyhow, it was a premature spring-like day, and he had left off his overcoat. That evening he went to the Odéon, and when, after the play, he joined us for supper at the Bleu, he said he thought he had caught a cold, and ordered hot grog. The next day he did not turn up at all; so several of us, after dinner, presented ourselves at his lodgings in Montparnasse. We found him in bed, with Nina reading to him. He was feverish, and Nina had insisted that he should stop at home. He would be all right to-morrow. He scoffed at our suggestion that he should see a doctor; he was one of those men who affect to despise the medical profession. But early on the following morning a commissionnaire brought me a note from Nina. "My father is very much worse. Can you come at once?" He was delirious. Poor Nina, white, with frightened eyes, moved about like one distracted. We sent off for Dr. Rénoult, we had in a Sister of Charity. Everything that could be done was done. Till the very end, none of us for a moment doubted that he would recover. It was impossible to conceive that that strong, affirmative life could be extinguished. And even after the end had come, the end with its ugly suite of material circumstances, I don't think any of us realized what it meant. It was as if we had been told that one of the forces of Nature had become inoperative. And Nina, through it all, was like some pale thing in marble, that breathed and moved: white, dazed, helpless, with aching, incredulous eyes, suffering everything, understanding nothing.

When it came to the worst of the dreadful necessary businesses that followed, some of us, somehow, managed to draw her from the death-chamber into another room, and to keep her there, while others of us got it over. It was snowing that afternoon, I remember, a melancholy, hesitating snowstorm, with large moist flakes that fluttered down irresolutely, and presently disintegrated into rain; but we had not far to go. Then we returned to Nina, and for many days and nights we never dared to leave her. You will guess whether the question of her future, especially of her immediate future, weighed heavily upon our minds. In the end, however, it appeared to have solved itself, — though I can't pretend that the solution was exactly all we could have wished.

Her father had a half-brother (we learned this from his papers), incumbent of rather an important living in the north of England. We also learned that the brothers had scarcely seen each other twice in a score of years, and had kept up only the most fitful correspondence. Nevertheless, we wrote to the clergyman, describing the sad case of his niece, and in reply we got a letter, addressed to Nina herself, saying that of course she must come at once to Yorkshire, and consider the rectory her home. I don't need to recount the difficulties we had in explaining to her, in persuading her. I have known few more painful moments than that when, at the Gare du Nord, half a dozen of us established the poor, benumbed, bewildered child in her compartment, and sent her, with our godspeed, alone upon her long journey — to her strange kindred, and the strange conditions of life she would have to encounter among them. From the Café Bleu to a Yorkshire parsonage! And Nina's was not by any means a neutral personality, nor her mind a blank sheet of paper. She had a will of her own; she had convictions, aspirations, traditions, prejudices, which she would hold to with enthusiasm because they had been her father's, because her father had taught them to her; and she had manners, habits, tastes. She would be sure to horrify the people she was going to; she would be sure to resent their criticism, their slightest attempt at interference. Oh, my heart was full of misgivings; yet — she had no money, she was eighteen years old — what else could we advise her to do? All the same, her face, as it looked down upon us from the window of her railway carriage, white, with big terrified eyes fixed in a gaze of blank uncomprehending anguish, kept rising up to reproach me for weeks afterwards. I had her on my conscience as if I had personally wronged her.

VI

It was characteristic of her that, during her absence, she hardly wrote to us. She is of far too hasty and impetuous a nature to take kindly to the task of letter-writing; her moods are too inconstant; her thoughts, her fancies, supersede one another too rapidly. Anyhow, beyond the telegram we had made her promise to send, announcing her safe arrival, the most favored of us got nothing more than an occasional scrappy note, if he got so much; while the greater number of the long epistles some of us felt in duty bound to address to her, elicited not even the semblance of an acknowledgment. Hence, about the particulars of her experience we were quite in the dark, though of its general features we were informed, succinctly, in a big, dashing, uncompromising hand, that she "hated" them.

VII

I am not sure whether it was late in April or early in May that Nina left us. But one day towards the middle of October, coming home from the restaurant where I had lunched, I found in my letter-box, in the concierge's room, two half sheets of paper, folded, with the corners turned down, and my name superscribed in pencil. The handwriting startled me a little — and yet, no, it was impossible. Then I hastened to unfold, and read, and of course it was the impossible which had happened.

"Mon cher, I am sorry not to find you at home, but I'll wait at the café at the corner till half-past twelve. It is now midi juste." That was the first. The second ran: "I have waited till a quarter to one. Now I am going to the Bleu for luncheon. I shall be there till three." And each was signed with the initials, N. C.

It was not yet two, so I had plenty of time. But you will believe that I didn't loiter on that account. I dashed out of the loge — into the street — down the Boulevard St. Michel — into the Bleu, breathlessly. At the far end Nina was seated before a marble table, with Madame Chanve in smiles and tears beside her. I heard a little cry; I felt myself seized and enveloped for a moment by something like a whirlwind — oh, but a very pleasant whirlwind, warm, and fresh, and fragrant of violets; I received two vigorous kisses, one on either cheek; and then I was held off at arm's length, and examined by a pair of laughing eyes.

And at last a voice — rather a deep voice for a woman's, with just a crisp edge to it, that might have been called slightly nasal, but was agreeable and individual — a voice said: "En voilà assez. Come and sit down."

She had finished her luncheon, and was taking

coffee; and if the whole truth must be told, I'm afraid she was taking it with a petit-verre and a cigarette. She wore an exceedingly simple black frock, with a bunch of violets in her breast, and a hat with a sweeping black feather and a daring brim. Her dark luxurious hair broke into a riot of fluffy little curls about her forehead, and thence waved richly away to where it was massed behind; her cheeks glowed with a lovely color (thanks, doubtless, to Yorkshire breezes: sweet are the uses of adversity); her eyes sparkled; her lips curved in a perpetual play of smiles, letting her delicate little teeth show themselves furtively; and suddenly I realized that this girl, whom I had never thought of save as one might think of one's younger sister, suddenly I realized that she was a woman, and a radiantly, perhaps even a dangerously, handsome woman. I saw suddenly that she was not merely an attribute, an aspect, of another, not merely Alfred Childe's daughter; she was a personage in herself, a personage to be reckoned with.

This sufficiently obvious perception came upon me with such force, and brought me such emotion, that I dare say for a little while I sat vacantly staring at her, with an air of preoccupation. Anyhow, all at once she laughed, and cried out, "Well, when you get back . . . ?" and, "Perhaps," she questioned, "perhaps you think it polite to go off wool-gathering like that?" Whereupon I recovered myself with a start, and laughed too.

"But say that you are surprised, say that you are glad, at least," she went on.

Surprised! glad! But what did it mean? What was it all about?

"I could n't stand it any longer, that's all. I have come home. Oh, que c'est bon, que c'est bon, que c'est bon!"

"And — England? — Yorkshire? — your people?"

"Don't speak of it. It was a bad dream. It is over. It brings bad luck to speak of bad dreams. I have forgotten it. I am here — in Paris — at home. Oh, que c'est bon!" And she smiled blissfully through eyes filled with tears.

Don't tell me that happiness is an illusion. It is her habit, if you will, to flee before us and elude us; but sometimes, sometimes we catch up with her, and can hold her for long moments warm against our hearts.

"Oh, mon père! It is enough — to be here, where he lived, where he worked, where he was happy," Nina murmured afterwards.

She had arrived the night before; she had taken a room in the Hôtel d'Espagne, in the Rue de Médicis, opposite the Luxembourg Garden. I was as yet the only member of the old set she had looked up. Of course I knew where she had gone first — but not to cry — to kiss it — to place flowers on it. She could not cry — not now. She was too happy, happy, happy. Oh, to be back in Paris, her home, where she had lived with him, where every stick and stone was dear to her because of him!

Then, glancing up at the clock, with an abrupt change of key, "Mais allons donc, paresseux! You must take me to see the camarades. You must take me to see Chalks."

And in the street she put her arm through mine, laughing, and saying, "On nous croira fiancés." She

did not walk, she tripped, she all but danced beside
me, chattering joyously in alternate French and English. "I could stop and kiss them all, — the men, the
women, the very pavement. Oh, Paris! Oh, these
good, gay, kind Parisians! Look at the sky! Look
at the view — down that impasse — the sunlight and
shadows on the houses, the doorways, the people.
Oh, the air! Oh, the smells! Que c'est bon — que
je suis contente! Et dire que j'ai passé cinq mois,
mais cinq grands mois, en Angleterre. Ah, veinard,
you — you don't know how you're blessed." Presently we found ourselves laboring knee-deep in a
wave of black pinafores, and Nina had plucked her
bunch of violets from her breast, and was dropping
them amongst eager fingers and rosy, cherubic smiles.
And it was constantly, "Tiens, there's Madame
Chose in her kiosque. Bonjour, madame. Vous allez
toujours bien?" and "Oh, look! old Perronet standing before his shop in his shirt-sleeves, exactly as he
has stood at this hour every day, winter or summer,
these ten years. Bonjour, M'sieu Perronet." And
you may be sure that the kindly French Choses and
Perronets returned her greetings with beaming faces.
"Ah, mademoiselle, que c'est bon de vous revoir
ainsi. Que vous avez bonne mine!" "It is so
strange," she said, "to find nothing changed. To
think that everything has gone on quietly in the
usual way. As if I hadn't spent an eternity in
exile!" And at the corner of one street, before a
vast flaunting "bazaar," with a prodigality of tawdry
Oriental wares exhibited on the pavement, and little
black shopmen trailing like beetles in and out
amongst them, "Oh," she cried, "the 'Mecque du

Quartier'! To think that I could weep for joy at seeing the 'Mecque du Quartier'!"

By and by we plunged into a dark hallway, climbed a long, unsavory, corkscrew staircase, and knocked at a door. A gruff voice having answered, "'Trez!" we entered Chalks's bare, bleak, paint-smelling studio. He was working (from a lay-figure) with his back towards us; and he went on working for a minute or two after our arrival, without speaking. Then he demanded, in a sort of grunt, "Eh bien, qu'est-ce que c'est?" always without pausing in his work or looking round. Nina gave two little *ahems*, tense with suppressed mirth; and slowly, indifferently, Chalks turned an absent-minded face in our direction. But, next instant, there was a shout — a rush — a confusion of forms in the middle of the floor — and I realized that I was not the only one to be honored by a kiss and an embrace. "Oh, you're covering me with paint," Nina protested suddenly; and indeed he had forgotten to drop his brush and palette, and great dabs of color were clinging to her cloak. While he was doing penance, scrubbing the garment with rags soaked in turpentine, he kept shaking his head, and murmuring, from time to time, as he glanced up at her, "Well, I'll be dumned."

"It's very nice and polite of you, Chalks," she said, by and by, "a very graceful concession to my sex. But, if you think it would relieve you once for all, you have my full permission to pronounce it — amned."

Chalks did no more work that afternoon; and that evening quite twenty of us dined at Madame Chanve's; and it was almost like old times.

VIII

"Oh, yes," she explained to me afterwards, "my uncle is a good man. My aunt and cousins are very good women. But for me to live with them, — pas possible, mon cher. Their thoughts were not my thoughts, we could not speak the same language. They disapproved of me unutterably. They suffered agonies, poor things. Oh, they were very kind, very patient. But—! My gods were their devils. My father — my great, grand, splendid father — was "poor Alfred," "poor uncle Alfred." Que voulez-vous? And then — the life, the society! The parishioners — the people who came to tea — the houses where we sometimes dined! Are you interested in crops? In the preservation of game? In the diseases of cattle? Olàlà! (C'est bien le cas de s'en servir, de cette expression-là.) Olàlà, làlà! And then — have you ever been homesick? Oh, I longed, I pined, for Paris, as one suffocating would long, would die, for air. Enfin, I could not stand it any longer. They thought it wicked to smoke cigarettes. My poor aunt — when she smelt cigarette-smoke in my bed-room! Oh, her face! I had to sneak away, behind the shrubbery at the end of the garden, for stealthy whiffs. And it was impossible to get French tobacco. At last I took the bull by the horns, and fled. It will have been a terrible shock for them. But better one good blow than endless little ones; better a lump-sum than instalments with interest."

But what was she going to do? How was she going to live? For, after all, much as she loved Paris, she could n't subsist on its air and sunshine.

Oh, never fear! I'll manage somehow. I'll not die of hunger," she said confidently.

IX

And, sure enough, she managed very well. She gave music lessons to the children of the Quarter, and English lessons to clerks and shop-girls; she did a little translating; she would pose now and then for a painter friend, — she was the original, for instance, of Norton's "Woman Dancing," which you know. She even — thanks to the employment by Chalks of what he called his "in*floo*ence" — she even contributed a weekly column of Paris gossip to the "Palladium," a newspaper published at Battle Creek, Michigan, U. S. A., Chalks's native town. "Put in lots about me, and talk as if there were only two important centres of civilization on earth, Battle Crick and Parus, and it'll be a boom," Chalks said. We used to have great fun concocting those columns of Paris gossip. Nina, indeed, held the pen and cast a deciding vote; but we all collaborated. And we put in lots about Chalks, — perhaps rather more than he had bargained for. With an irony (we trusted) too subtle to be suspected by the good people of Battle Creek, we would introduce their illustrious fellow-citizen, casually, between the Pope and the President of the Republic; we would sketch him as he strolled in the Boulevard arm-in-arm with Monsieur Meissonier, as he dined with the Perpetual Secretary of the French Academy, or drank his bock in the afternoon with the Grand Chancellor of the Legion of Honor; we would compose solemn descriptive criticisms of his works, which almost made us die of laughing; we would interview him — at length — about any subject; we would give elaborate bulletins of his health, and brilliant pen-pictures of his toilets. Sometimes we would betroth him, marry him, divorce him; sometimes, when our muse impelled us to a particularly daring flight, we would insinuate, darkly, sorrowfully, that perhaps the great man's morals . . . but no! We were persuaded that rumor accused him falsely. The story that he had been seen dancing at Bullier's with the notorious Duchesse de Z—— was a baseless fabrication. Unprincipled? Oh, we were nothing if not unprincipled. And our pleasure was so exquisite, and it worried our victim so. "I suppose you think it's funny, don't you?" he used to ask, with a feint of superior scorn which put its fine flower to our hilarity. "Look out, or you'll bust," he would warn us, the only unconvulsed member present. "By gum, you're easily amused." We always wrote of him respectfully as Mr. Charles K. Smith; we never faintly hinted at his sobriquet. We would have rewarded liberally, at that time, any one who could have told us what the K. stood for. We yearned to unite the cryptic word to his surname by a hyphen; the mere abstract notion of doing so filled us with fearful joy. Chalks was right, I dare say; we were easily amused. And Nina, at these moments of literary frenzy — I can see her now: her head bent over the manuscript, her hair in some disarray, a spiral of cigarette-smoke winding ceilingward from between the fingers of her idle hand, her lips parted, her eyes gleaming with mischievous inspirations, her face pale with the intensity of her glee.

I can see her as she would look up, eagerly, to listen to somebody's suggestion, or as she would motion to us to be silent, crying, "Attendez — I've got an idea." Then her pen would dash swiftly, noisily, over her paper for a little, whilst we all waited expectantly; and at last she would lean back, drawing a long breath, and tossing the pen aside, to read her paragraph out to us.

In a word, she managed very well, and by no means died of hunger. She could scarcely afford Madame Chanve's three-franc table d'hôte, it is true; but we could dine modestly at Léon's, over the way, and return to the Bleu for coffee; though, it must be added, that establishment no longer enjoyed a monopoly of our custom. We patronized it and the Vachette, the Source, the Ecoles, the Souris, indifferently. Or we would sometimes spend our evenings in Nina's rooms. She lived in a tremendously swagger house in the Avenue de l'Observatoire, — on the sixth floor, to be sure, but "there was a carpet all the way up." She had a charming little salon, with her own furniture and piano (the same that had formerly embellished our café), and no end of books, pictures, draperies, and pretty things, inherited from her father or presented by her friends.

By this time the inevitable had happened, and we were all in love with her, — hopelessly, resignedly so, and without internecine rancor; for she treated us, indiscriminately, with a serene, impartial, tolerant derision; but we were savagely, luridly, jealous and suspicious of all new-comers and of all outsiders. If *we* could not win her, no one else should; and we formed ourselves round her in a ring of fire. Oh, the maddening, mock-sentimental, mock-sympathetic face she would pull when one of us ventured to sigh to her of his passion! The way she would lift her eyebrows and gaze at you with a travesty of pity, shaking her head pensively, and murmuring, "Mon pauvre ami! Only fancy!" And then how the imp, lurking in the corners of her eyes, with only the barest pretence of trying to conceal himself, would suddenly leap forth in a peal of laughter!. She had lately read Mr. Howells's "Undiscovered Country," and had adopted the Shakers' paraphrase for love: "Feeling foolish." — "Feeling pretty foolish to-day, air ye, gentlemen?" she inquired, mimicking the dialect of Chalks. "Well, I guess you just ain't feeling any more foolish than you look." — If she would but have taken us seriously! And the worst of it was that we knew she was anything but temperamentally cold. Chalks formulated the potentialities we divined in her, when he remarked, regretfully, wistfully, as he often did, "She could love like Hell." Once, in a reckless moment, he even went so far as to tell her this point-blank. "Oh, naughty Chalks!" she remonstrated, shaking her finger at him. "Do you think that's a pretty word? But — I dare say I could."

"All the same, Lord help the man you marry," Chalks continued gloomily.

"Oh, I shall never marry," Nina cried. "Because, first, I don't approve of matrimony as an institution. And then — as you say — Lord help my husband. I should be such an uncomfortable wife. So capricious, and flighty, and tantalizing, and unsettling, and disobedient, and exacting, and everything. Oh, but a horrid wife! No, I shall never marry. Marriage is quite too out-of-date. I sha'n't marry; but if I ever meet a man and love him — ah!" She placed two fingers upon her lips, and kissed them, and waved the kiss to the skies.

This fragment of conversation passed in the Luxembourg Garden; and the three or four of us by whom she was accompanied glared threateningly at our mental image of that not-impossible upstart whom she might some day meet and love. We were sure, of course, that he would be a beast; we hated him not merely because he would have cut us out with her, but because he would be so distinctly our inferior, so hopelessly unworthy of her, so helplessly incapable of appreciating her. I think we conceived of him as tall, with drooping fair moustaches, and contemptibly meticulous in his dress. He would probably not be of the Quarter; he would sneer at *us*.

"He'll not understand her, he'll not respect her. Take her peculiar views. We know where she gets them. But he — he'll despise her for them, at the very time he's profiting by 'em," some one said.

Her peculiar views of the institution of matrimony, the speaker meant. She had got them from her father. "The relations of the sexes should be as free as friendship," he had taught. "If a man and a woman love each other, it is nobody's business but their own. Neither the Law nor Society can, with any show of justice, interfere. That they do interfere, is a survival of feudalism, a survival of the system under which the individual, the subject, had no liberty, no rights. If a man and a woman love each other, they should be as free to determine for themselves the character, extent, and duration of their intercourse, as two friends should be. If they wish to live together under the same roof, let them. If they wish to retain their separate domiciles, let them. If they wish to cleave to each other till death severs them — if they wish to part on the morrow of their union — let them, by heaven. But the couple who go before a priest or a magistrate, and bind themselves in ceremonial marriage, are serving to perpetuate tyranny, are insulting the dignity of human nature." Such was the gospel which Nina had absorbed (don't, for goodness' sake, imagine that I approve of it because I cite it), and which she professed in entire good faith. We felt that the coming man would misapprehend both it and her — though he would not hesitate to make a convenience of it. Ugh, the cynic!

We formed ourselves round her in a ring of fire, hoping to frighten the beast away. But we were miserably, fiercely anxious, suspicious, jealous. We were jealous of everything in the shape of a man that came into any sort of contact with her: of the men who passed her in the street or rode with her in the omnibus; of the little employés de commerce to whom she gave English lessons; of everybody. I fancy we were always more or less uneasy in our minds when she was out of our sight. Who could tell what might be happening? With those lips of hers, those eyes of hers — oh, we knew how she could love: Chalks had said it. Who could tell what might already have happened? Who could tell that the coming man had not already come? She was entirely capable of concealing him from us. Sometimes, in the evening, she would seem absent, preoccupied. How could we be sure that she wasn't thinking of him? Savoring anew the hours she had passed with him that very day? Or dreaming of those she had promised him for to-morrow? If she took leave of us — might he not be waiting to join her round the corner? If she spent an evening away from us. . . .

And she — she only laughed; laughed at our jealousy, our fears, our precautions, as she laughed at our hankering flame. Not a laugh that reassured us, though; an inscrutable, enigmatic laugh, that might have covered a multitude of sins. She had taken to calling us collectively *Loulou*. "Ah, le pauv' Loulou — so now he has the pretension to be jealous." Then she would be interrupted by a paroxysm of laughter; after which, "Oh, qu'il est drôle," she would gasp. "Pourvu qu'il ne devienne pas gênant!"

It was all very well to laugh; but some of us, our personal equation quite apart, could not help feeling that the joke was of a precarious quality, that the situation held tragic possibilities. A young and attractive girl, by no means constitutionally insusceptible, and imbued with heterodox ideas of marriage — alone in the Latin Quarter.

X

I have heard it maintained that the man has yet to be born, who, in his heart of hearts, if he comes to think the matter over, won't find himself at something of a loss to conceive why any given woman should experience the passion of love for any other man; that a woman's choice, to all men save the chosen, is, by its very nature, as incomprehensible as

the postulates of Hegel. But, in Nina's case, even
when I regard it from this distance of time, I still
feel, as we all felt then, that the mystery was more
than ordinarily obscure. We had fancied ourselves
prepared for anything; the only thing we were n't
prepared for was the thing that befell. We had
expected "him" to be offensive, and he was n't. He
was, quite simply, insignificant. He was a South
American, a Brazilian, a member of the School of
Mines: a poor, undersized, pale, spiritless, apologetic
creature, with rather a Teutonic-looking name, Ernest
Mayer. His father, or uncle, was Minister of Agriculture, or Commerce, or something, in his native
land; and he himself was attached in some nominal
capacity to the Brazilian Legation, in the Rue de Téhéran, whence, on state occasions, he enjoyed the privilege of enveloping his meagre little person in a very
gorgeous diplomatic uniform. He was beardless, with
vague features, timid, light-blue eyes, and a bluish,
anæmic skin. In manner he was nervous, tremulous, deprecatory — perpetually bowing, wriggling,
stepping back to let you pass, waving his hands,
palms outward, as if to protest against giving you
trouble. And in speech — upon my word, I don't
think I ever heard him compromise himself by any
more dangerous assertion than that the weather was
fine, or he wished you good-day. For the most part he
listened mutely, with a flickering, perfunctory smile.
From time to time, with an air of casting fear behind
him and dashing into the imminent deadly breach, he
would hazzard an "Ah, oui," or a "Pas mal." For
the rest, he played the piano prettily enough, wrote
colorless, correct French verse, and was reputed to be

an industrious if not a brilliant student,— what we called *un sérieux.*

It was hard to believe that beautiful, sumptuous Nina Childe, with her wit, her humor, her imagination, loved this neutral little fellow; yet she made no secret of doing so. We tried to frame a theory that would account for it. "It's the maternal instinct," suggested one. "It's her chivalry," said another; "she's the sort of woman who could never be very violently interested by a man of her own size. She would need one she could look up to, or else one she could protect and pat on the head." "'God be thanked, the meanest of His creatures boasts two soul-sides, one to face the world with, one to show a woman when he loves her,'" quoted a third. "Perhaps Coco"— we had nicknamed him Coco — "has luminous qualities that we don't dream of, to which he gives the rein when they 're à deux."

Anyhow, if we were mortified that she should have preferred such a one to us, we were relieved to think that she had n't fallen into the clutches of a blackguard, as we had feared she would. That Coco was a blackguard we never guessed. We made the best of him, because we had to choose between doing that and seeing less of Nina: in time, I am afraid — such is the influence of habit — we rather got to like him, as one gets to like any innocuous customary thing. And if we did not like the situation — for none of us, whatever might have been our practice, shared Nina's hereditary theories anent the sexual conventions — we recognized that we could n't alter it, and we shrugged our shoulders resignedly, trusting it might be no worse.

And then one day she announced, "Ernest and I are going to be married." And when we cried out why, she explained that — despite her own conviction that marriage was a barbarous institution — she felt, in the present state of public opinion, people owed legitimacy to their children. So Ernest, who, according to both French and Brazilian law, could not, at his age, marry without his parents' consent, was going home to procure it. He would sail next week; he would be back before three months. Ernest sailed from Lisbon; and the post, a day or two after he was safe at sea, brought Nina a letter from him. It was a wild, hysterical, remorseful letter, in which he called himself every sort of name. He said his parents would never dream of letting him marry her. They were Catholics, they were very devout, they had prejudices, they had old-fashioned notions. Besides, he had been as good as affianced to a lady of their election ever since he was born. He was going home to marry his second cousin.

XI

Shortly after the birth of Camille I had to go to London, and it was nearly a year before I came back to Paris. Nina was looking better than when I had left, but still in nowise like her old self, — pale and worn and worried, with a smile that was the ghost of her former one. She had been waiting for my return, she said, to have a long talk with me. "I have made a little plan. I want you to advise me. Of course you must advise me to stick to it."

And when we had reached her lodgings, and were alone in the salon, "It is about Camille, it is about her bringing-up," she explained. "The Latin Quarter? It is all very well for you, for me; but for a growing child? Oh, my case was different; I had my father. But Camille? Restaurants, cafés, studios, the Boul' Miche, and this little garret — do they form a wholesome environment? Oh, no, no — I am not a renegade. I am a Bohemian; I shall always be; it is bred in the bone. But my daughter — ought she not to have the opportunity, at least, of being different, of being like other girls? You see, I had my father; she will have only me. And I distrust myself; I have no 'system.' Shall I not do better, then, to adopt the system of the world? To give her the conventional education, the conventional 'advantages'? A home, what they call home influences. Then, when she has grown up, she can choose for herself. Besides, there is the question of francs and centimes. I have been able to earn a living for myself, it is true. But even that is more difficult now; I can give less time to work; I am in debt. And we are two; and our expenses must naturally increase from year to year. And I should like to be able to put something aside. Hand-to-mouth is a bad principle when you have a growing child."

After a little pause she went on, "So my problem is, first, how to earn our livelihood, and secondly, how to make something like a home for Camille, something better than this tobacco-smoky, absinthe-scented atmosphere of the Latin Quarter. And I can see only one way of accomplishing the two things. You will smile — but I have considered it from every point of view. I have examined myself, my own capabilities. I have weighed all the chances. I wish to take a flat, in another quarter of the town, near the Etoile or the Parc Monceau, and — open a pension. There is my plan."

I had a much simpler and pleasanter plan of my own, but of that, as I knew, she would hear nothing. I did not smile at hers, however; though I confess it was not easy to imagine madcap Nina in the rôle of a landlady, regulating the accounts and presiding at the table of a boarding-house. I can't pretend that I believed there was the slightest likelihood of her filling it with success. But I said nothing to discourage her; and the fact that she is rich to-day proves how little I divined the resources of her character. For the boarding-house she kept was an exceedingly good boarding-house; she showed herself the most practical of mistresses; and she prospered amazingly. Jeanselme, whose father had recently died, leaving him a fortune, lent her what money she needed to begin with; she took and furnished a flat in the Avenue de l'Alma; and I — I feel quite like an historical personage when I remember that I was her first boarder. Others soon followed me, though, for she had friends amongst all the peoples of the earth, — English and Americans, Russians, Italians, Austrians, even Roumanians and Servians, as well as French; and each did what he could to help. At the end of a year she overflowed into the flat above; then into that below; then she acquired the lease of the entire house. She worked tremendously, she was at it early and late, her eyes were everywhere. She set an excellent table; she employed admirable servants;

and if her prices were a bit stiff, she gave you your money's worth, and there were no "surprises." It was comfortable and quiet; the street was bright; the neighborhood convenient. You could dine in the common salle-à-manger if you liked, or in your private sitting-room. And you never saw your landlady except for purposes of business. She lived apart, in the entresol, alone with Camille and her body-servant, Jeanne. There was the "home" she had set out to make.

Meanwhile another sort of success was steadily thrusting itself upon her,—she certainly never went out of her way to seek it; she was much too busy to do that. Such of her old friends as remained in Paris came frequently to see her, and new friends gathered round her. She was beautiful, she was intelligent, responsive, entertaining. In her salon, on a Friday evening, you would meet half the lions that were at large in the town,—authors, painters, actors, actresses, deputies, even an occasional Cabinet minister. Red ribbons and red rosettes shone from every corner of the room. She had become one of the oligarchs of la haute Bohème, she had become one of the celebrities of Paris. It would be tiresome to count the novels, poems, songs, that were dedicated to her, the portraits of her, painted or sculptured, that appeared at the Mirlitons or the Palais de l'Industrie. Numberless were the partis who asked her to marry them (I know one, at least, who has returned to the charge again and again), but she only laughed, and vowed she would never marry. I don't say that she has never had her fancies, her experiences; but she has consistently scoffed at marriage. At any rate, she has never affected the least repentance for what some people would call her "fault." Her ideas of right and wrong have undergone very little modification. She was deceived in her estimate of the character of Ernest Mayer, if you please; but she would indignantly deny that there was anything sinful, anything to be ashamed of, in her relations with him. And if, by reason of them, she at one time suffered a good deal of pain, I am sure she accounts Camille an exceeding great compensation. That Camille is her child she would scorn to make a secret. She has scorned to assume the conciliatory title of Madame. As plain Mademoiselle, with a daughter, you must take her or leave her. And, somehow, all this has not seemed to make the faintest difference to her clientèle, not even to the primmest of the English. I can't think of one of them who did not treat her with deference, like her, and recommend her house.

But *her* house they need recommend no more, for she has sold it. Last spring, when I was in Paris, she told me she was about to do so. "Ouf! I have lived with my nose to the grindstone long enough. I am going to 'retire.'" What money she had saved from season to season, she explained, she had entrusted to her friend Baron C * * * * * for speculation. "He is a wizard, and so I am a rich woman. I shall have an income of something like three thousand pounds, mon cher! Oh, we will roll in it. I have had ten bad years — ten hateful years. You don't know how I have hated it all, this business, this drudgery, this cut-and-dried, methodical existence, — moi, enfant de Bohème! But, enfin, it was obligatory. Now we will change all that. Nous reviendrons à nos premières amours. I shall have ten good years, — ten years of barefaced pleasure. Then — I will range myself — perhaps. There is the darlingest little house for sale, a sort of châlet, built of red brick, with pointed windows and things, in the Rue de Lisbonne. I shall buy it — furnish it — decorate it. Oh, you will see. I shall have my carriage, I shall have toilets, I shall entertain, I shall give dinners — olàlà! No more boarders, no more bores, cares, responsibilities. Only my friends and — *life!* I feel like one emerging from ten years in the galleys, ten years of penal servitude. To the Pension Childe — bonsoir!"

"That's all very well for you," her listener complained sombrely. "But for me? Where shall I stop when I come to Paris?"

"With me. You shall be my guest. I will kill you if you ever go elsewhere. You shall pass your old age in a big chair in the best room, and Camille and I will nurse your gout and make herb-tea for you."

"And I shall sit and think of what might have been."

"Yes, we'll indulge all your little foibles. You shall sit and 'feel foolish' — from dawn to dewy eve."

XII

If you had chanced to be walking in the Bois-de-Boulogne this afternoon, you might have seen a smart little basket-phaeton flash past, drawn by two glossy bays, and driven by a woman, — a woman with sparkling eyes, a lovely color, great quantities of soft dark hair, and a figure —

"Hélas, mon père, la taille d'une déesse "—

a smiling woman, in a wonderful blue-gray toilet, gray driving-gloves, and a bold-brimmed gray-felt hat with waving plumes. And in the man beside her you would have recognized your servant. You would have thought me in great luck, perhaps you would have envied me. But — esse, quam videri! — I would I were as enviable as I looked.

MERCEDES.

MERCEDES.

WHEN I was a child some one gave me a family of white mice. I don't remember how old I was, I think about ten or eleven; but I remember very clearly the day I received them. It must have been a Thursday, a half-holiday, for I had come home from school rather early in the afternoon. Alexandre, dear old ruddy round-faced Alexandre, who opened the door for me, smiled in a way that seemed to announce, "There's a surprise in store for you, sir." Then my mother smiled too, a smile, I thought, of peculiar promise and interest. After I had kissed her she said, "Come into the dining-room. There's something you will like." Perhaps I concluded it would be something to eat. Anyhow, all agog with curiosity, I followed her into the dining-room — and Alexandre followed *me*, anxious to take part in the rejoicing. In the window stood a big cage, enclosing the family of white mice.

I remember it as a very big cage indeed; no doubt, I should find it shrunken to quite moderate dimensions if I could see it again. There were three generations of mice in it, — a fat old couple, the founders of the race, dozing phlegmatically on their laurels in a corner; then a dozen medium-sized, slender mice, trim and youthful-looking, rushing irrelevantly hither and thither, with funny inquisitive little faces; and then a squirming mass of pink things, like caterpillars, that were really infant mice, new-born. They did n't remain infants long, though. In a few days they had put on virile togas of white fur, and were scrambling about the cage, and nibbling their food as independently as their elders. The rapidity with which my mice multiplied and grew to maturity was a constant source of astonishment to me. It seemed as if every morning I found a new litter of young mice in the cage,—though how they had effected an entrance through the wire gauze that lined it was a hopeless puzzle,—and these would have become responsible, self-supporting mice in no time.

My mother told me that somebody had sent me this soul-stirring present from the country, and I dare say I was made to sit down and write a letter of thanks. But I 'm ashamed to own I can't remember who the giver was. I have a vague notion that it was a lady, an elderly maiden-lady—Mademoiselle . . . something that began with P—who lived near Tours, and who used to come to Paris once or twice a year, and always brought me a box of prunes.

Alexandre carried the cage into my play-room, and set it up against the wall. I stationed myself in front of it, and remained there all the rest of the afternoon, gazing in, entranced. To watch their antics, their comings and goings, their labors and amusements, to study their shrewd, alert physiognomies, to wonder about their feelings, thoughts, intentions, to try to divine the meaning of their busy twittering language,—it was such keen, deep delight. Of course I was an anthropomorphist, and read a great deal of human nature into them; otherwise it would n't have been such fun. I dragged myself reluctantly away when I was called to dinner. It was hard that evening to apply myself to my school-books. Before I went to bed I paid them a parting visit; they were huddled together in their nest of cotton-wool, sleeping soundly. And I was up at an unheard-of hour next morning, to have a bout with them before going to school. I found Alexandre, in his nightcap and long white apron, occupied with the soins de propreté, as he said. He cleaned out the cage, put in fresh food and water, and then, pointing to the fat old couple, the grandparents, who stopped lazily abed, sitting up and rubbing their noses together, whilst their juniors scampered merrily about their affairs, "Tiens! On dirait Monsieur et Madame Denis," he cried. I felt the appositeness of his allusion; and the old couple were forthwith officially denominated Monsieur and Madame Denis, for their resemblance to the hero and heroine of the song; though which was Monsieur, and which Madame, I'm not sure that I ever clearly knew.

It was a little after this that I was taken for the first time in my life to the play. I fancy the theatre must have been the Porte St. Martin; at any rate, it was a theâtre in the Boulevard, and towards the East, for I remember the long drive we had to reach it. And the piece was "The Count of Monte Cristo." In my memory the adventure shines, of course, as a vague blur of light and joy; a child's first visit to the play, and that play "The Count of Monte Cristo!" It was all the breath-taking pleasantness of romance made visible, audible, actual. A vague blur of light and joy, from which only two details separate themselves. First, the prison scene, and an aged man, with a long white beard, moving a great stone from the wall; then — the figure of Mercedes. I went home terribly in love with Mercedes. Surely there are no such grandes passions in maturer life as those helpless, inarticulate ones we burn in secret with, before our teens; surely we never love again so violently, desperately, consumedly. Anyhow, I went home terribly in love with Mercedes. And — do all children lack humor? — I picked out the prettiest young ladyish-looking mouse in my collection, cut off her moustaches, adopted her as my especial pet, and called her by the name of my dea certe.

All of my mice by this time had become quite tame. They had plenty to eat and drink, and a comfortable home, and not a care in the world; and familiarity with their master had bred assurance; and so they had become quite tame, and shamefully, abominably lazy. Luxury, we are taught, was ever the mother of sloth. I could put my hand in amongst them, and not one would bestir himself the littlest bit to escape me. Mercedes and I were inseparable. I used to take her to school with me every day; she could be more conveniently and privately transported than a lamb. Each lycéen had a desk in front of his form, and she would spend the school-hours in mine, I leaving the lid raised a little, that she might have light and air. One day, the usher having left the room for a moment, I put her down on the floor, thereby creating a great excitement amongst my fellow-pupils, who got up from their places and formed an eager circle round her. Then suddenly the usher came back, and we all hurried to our seats, while he, catching sight of Mercedes, cried out, "A mouse! A white mouse! Who dares to bring a white mouse to the class?" And he made a dash for her. But she was too quick, too 'cute, for "the likes of" Monsieur le Pion. She gave a jump, and in the twinkling of an eye had disappeared up my leg, under my trousers. The usher searched high and low for her, but she prudently remained in her hiding-place; and thus her life was saved, for, when he had abandoned his ineffectual chase, he announced, "I should have wrung her neck." I turned pale to imagine the doom she had escaped as by a hair's-breadth. "It is useless to ask which of you brought her here," he continued. "But mark my words: if ever I find a mouse again in the class *I will wring her neck!*" And yet, in private life, this bloodthirsty *pion* was a quite gentle, kindly, underfed, underpaid, shabby, struggling fellow, with literary aspirations, who would not have hurt a fly.

The secrets of a schoolboy's pocket! I once saw a boy surreptitiously angling in Kensington Gardens, with a string and a bent pin. Presently he landed a fish, a fish no bigger than your thumb perhaps, but still a fish. Alive and wet and flopping as it was, he slipped it into his pocket. I used to carry Mercedes about in mine. One evening, when I put in my hand to take her out, I discovered to my bewilderment that she was not alone. There were four little pink mites of infant mice clinging to her.

I had enjoyed my visit to the theatre so much that at the jour de l'an my father included a toy-theatre among my presents. It had a real curtain of green baize, that would roll up and down, and beautiful colored scenery that you could shift, and footlights, and a trap-door in the middle of the stage; and indeed it would have been altogether perfect, except for the Company. I have since learned that this is not infrequently the case with theatres. My company consisted of pasteboard men and women who, as artists, struck me as eminently unsatisfactory. They could n't move their arms or legs, and they had such stolid, uninteresting faces. I don't know how it first occurred to me to turn them all off, and fill their places with my mice. Mercedes, of course, was leading lady; Monsieur and Madame Denis were the heavy parents; and a gentlemanlike young mouse named Leander was jeune premier. Then, in my leisure, they used to act the most tremendous plays. I was stage-manager, prompter, playwright, chorus, and audience, placing the theatre before a looking-glass, so that, though my duties kept me behind, I could peer round the edge, and watch the spectacle as from the front. I would invent the lines and deliver them; but, that my illusion might be the more complete, I would change my voice for each personage. The lines tried hard to be verses; no doubt they were vers libres. At any rate, they were mouth-filling and sonorous. The first play we attempted, I need hardly say, was "Le Comte de Monte Cristo," such version of it as I could reconstruct from memory. That had rather a long run. Then I dramatized "Aladdin and the Wonderful Lamp," "Paul et Virginie," "Quentin Durward," and "La Dame de Monsoreau." Mercedes made a charming Diane, Leander a brilliant and dashing Bussy; Monsieur Denis was cast for the rôle of Frère Gorenflot; and a long, thin, cadaverous-looking mouse, Don Quichotte by name, somewhat inadequately represented Chicot. We began, as you see, with melodrama; presently we descended to light comedy, playing "Les Mémoires d'un Ane," "Jean qui rit," and other works of the immortal Madame de Ségur. And then at last we turned a new leaf, and became naturalistic. We had never heard of the naturalist school, though Monsieur Zola had already published some volumes of the "Rougon-Macquart;" but ideas are in the air; and we, for ourselves, discovered the possibilities of naturalism simultaneously, as it were, with the acknowledged apostle of that form of art. We would impersonate the characters of our own world — our schoolfellows and masters, our parents, servants, friends — and carry them through experiences and situations derived from our impressions of real life. Perhaps we rather led them a dance; and I dare say those we did n't like came in for a good deal of retributive justice. It was a little universe, of which we were the arch-arbiters, our will the final law.

I don't know whether all children lack humor; but I 'm sure no grown-up author-manager can take his business more seriously than I took mine. Oh, I enjoyed it hugely; the hours I spent at it were enraptured hours; but it was grim, grim earnest. After a while I began to long for a less subjective public, a more various audience. I would summon the servants, range them in chairs at one end of the room, conceal myself behind the theatre, and spout the play with fervid solemnity. And they would giggle, and make flippant commentaries, and at my most impassioned climaxes burst into guffaws. My mice, as has been said, were overfed and lazy, and I used to have to poke them through their parts with sticks from the wings; but this was a detail which a superior imagination should have accepted as one of the conventions of the art. It made the servants laugh, however; and when I would step to the front in person, and, with tears in my eyes, beseech them to be sober, they would but laugh the louder. "Bless you, sir, they're only mice — ce- ne sont que des souris," the cook called out on one such occasion. She meant it as an apology and a consolation, but it was the unkindest cut of all. Only mice, indeed! To me they had been a young gentleman and lady lost in the Desert of Sahara, near to die for the want of water, and about to be attacked, captured, and sold into slavery by a band of Bedouin Arabs. Ah, well, the artist must steel himself to meet with indifference or derision from the public, to be ignored, misunderstood, or jeered at; and to rely for his real, his legitimate reward on the pleasure he finds in his work.

And now there befell a great change in my life. Our home in Paris was broken up, and we moved to St. Petersburg. It was impossible to take my mice with us; their cage would have hopelessly complicated our impedimenta. So we gave them to the children of our concierge. Mercedes, however, I was resolved I would not part with, and I carried her all the way to the Russian capital by hand. In my heart I was looking to her to found another family, — she had so frequently become a mother in the past. But month succeeded month, and she forever disappointed me, and at last I abandoned hope. In solitude and exile Mercedes degenerated sadly; got monstrously fat; too indolent to gnaw, let her teeth grow to a preposterous length; and in the end died of a surfeit of smetana.

When I returned to Paris, at the age of twenty, to faire mon droit in the Latin Quarter, I paid a visit to our old house, and discovered the same old concierge in the loge. I asked her about the mice, and she told me her children had found the care of them such a bother that at first they had neglected them, and at last allowed them to escape. "They took to the walls, and for a long time afterwards, Monsieur, the mice of this neighborhood were pied. To this day they are of a paler hue than elsewhere."

A BROKEN LOOKING-GLASS.

A BROKEN LOOKING-GLASS.

HE climbed the three flights of stone stairs, and put his key into the lock; but before he turned it, he stopped — to rest, to take breath. On the door his name was painted in big white letters, MR. RICHARD DANE. It is always silent in the Temple at midnight; to-night the silence was dense, like a fog. It was Sunday night; and on Sunday night, even within the hushed precincts of the Temple, one is conscious of a deeper hush.

When he had lighted the lamp in his sitting-room, he let himself drop into an arm-chair before the empty fireplace. He was tired, he was exhausted. Yet nothing had happened to tire him. He had dined, as he always dined on Sundays, with the Rodericks, in Cheyne Walk; he had driven home in a hansom. There was no reason why he should be tired. But he was tired. A deadly lassitude penetrated his body and his spirit, like a fluid. He was too tired to go to bed.

"I suppose I am getting old," he thought.

To a second person the matter would have appeared not one of supposition, but of certainty, not of progression, but of accomplishment. Getting old, indeed? But he *was* old. It was an old man, gray and wrinkled and wasted, who sat there, limp, sunken upon himself, in his easy-chair. In years, to be sure, he was under sixty; but he looked like a man of seventy-five.

"I am getting old, I suppose I am getting old."

And vaguely, dully, he contemplated his life, spread out behind him like a misty landscape, and thought what a failure it had been. What had it come to? What had it brought him? What had he done or won? Nothing, nothing. It had brought him nothing but old age, solitude, disappointment, and, to-night especially, a sense of fatigue and apathy that weighed upon him like a suffocating blanket. On a table, a yard or two away, stood a decanter of whiskey, with some soda-water bottles and tumblers; he looked at it with heavy eyes, and he knew that there was what he needed. A little whiskey would strengthen him, revive him, and make it possible for him to bestir himself and undress and go to bed. But when he thought of rising, and moving to pour the whiskey out, he shrank from that effort as from an Herculean labor; no — he was too tired. Then his mind went back to the friends he had left in Chelsea half an hour ago; it seemed an indefinably long time ago, years and years ago; they were like blurred phantoms, dimly remembered from a remote past.

Yes, his life had been a failure; total, miserable, abject. It had come to nothing; its harvest was a harvest of ashes. If it had been a useful life, he could have accepted its unhappiness; if it had been a happy life, he could have forgiven its uselessness; but it had been both useless and unhappy. He had done nothing for others, he had won nothing for himself. Oh, but he had tried, he had tried. When he had left Oxford, people expected great things of him;

he had expected great things of himself. He was admitted to be clever, to be gifted; he was ambitious, he was in earnest. He wished to make a name, he wished to justify his existence by fruitful work. And he had worked hard. He had put all his knowledge, all his talent, all his energy into his work; he had not spared himself; he had passed laborious days and studious nights. And what remained to show for it? Three or four volumes upon Political Economy, that had been read in their day a little, discussed a little, and then quite forgotten, — superseded by the books of newer men. "Pulped, pulped," he reflected bitterly. Except for a stray dozen of copies scattered here and there, — in the British Museum, in his College library, on his own bookshelves, — his published writings had by this time (he could not doubt) met with the common fate of unappreciated literature, and been "pulped."

"Pulped — pulped; pulped — pulped." The hateful word beat rhythmically again and again in his tired brain; and for a little while that was all he was conscious of.

So much for the work of his life. And for the rest? The play? The living? Oh, he had nothing to recall but failure. It had sufficed that he should desire a thing, for him to miss it; that he should set his heart upon a thing, for it to be removed beyond the sphere of his possible acquisition. It had been so from the beginning; it had been so always. He sat motionless as a stone, and allowed his thoughts to drift listlessly hither and thither in the current of memory. Everywhere they encountered wreckage, derelicts; defeated aspirations, broken hopes. Languidly he envisaged these. He was too tired to resent, to rebel. He even found a certain sluggish satisfaction in recognizing with what unvarying harshness destiny had treated him, in resigning himself to the unmerited.

He caught sight of his hand, lying flat and inert upon the brown leather arm of his chair. His eyes rested on it, and for the moment he forgot everything else in a sort of torpid study of it. How white it was, how thin, how withered; the nails were parched into minute corrugations; the veins stood out like dark wires; the skin hung loosely on it, and had a dry lustre: an old man's hand. He gazed at it fixedly, till his eyes closed and his head fell forward. But he was not sleepy, he was only tired and weak.

He raised his head with a start, and changed his position. He felt cold; but to endure the cold was easier than to get up and put something on, or go to bed.

How silent the world was; how empty his room. An immense feeling of solitude, of isolation, fell upon him. He was quite cut off from the rest of humanity here. If anything should happen to him, if he should need help of any sort, what could he do? Call out? But who would hear? At nine in the morning the porter's wife would come with his tea. But if anything should happen to him in the mean time? There would be nothing for it but to wait till nine o'clock.

Ah, if he had married, if he had had children, a wife, a home of his own, instead of these desolate bachelor chambers!

If he had married, indeed! It was his sorrow's crown of sorrow that he had not married, that he had not been able to marry, that the girl he had wished to marry would n't have him. Failure? Success? He could have accounted failure in other things a trifle, he could have laughed at what the world calls failure, if Elinor Lynd had been his wife. But that was the heart of his misfortune, she would n't have him.

He had met her for the first time when he was a lad of twenty, and she a girl of eighteen. He could see her palpable before him now: her slender girlish figure, her bright eyes, her laughing mouth, her warm brown hair curling round her forehead. Oh, how he had loved her. For twelve years he had waited upon her, wooed her, hoped to win her. But she had always said, "No — I don't love you. I am very fond of you; I love you as a friend; we all love you that way, — my mother, my father, my sisters. But I can't marry you." However, she married no one else, she loved no one else; and for twelve years he was an ever-welcome guest in her father's house; and she would talk with him, play to him, pity him; and he could hope. Then she died. He called one day, and they said she was ill. After that there came a blank in his memory, — a gulf, full of blackness and redness, anguish and confusion; and then a sort of dreadful sudden calm, when they told him she was dead.

He remembered standing in her room, after the funeral, with her father, her mother, her sister Elizabeth. He remembered the pale daylight that filled it, and how orderly and cold and forsaken it all looked. And there was her bed, the bed she had died in; and there her dressing-table, with her combs and brushes; and there her writing-desk, her book-case.

He remembered a row of medicine bottles on the mantelpiece; he remembered the fierce anger, the hatred of them, as if they were animate, that had welled up in his heart as he looked at them, because they had failed to do their work.

"You will wish to have something that was hers, Richard," her mother said. "What would you like?"

On her dressing-table there was a small looking-glass, in an ivory frame. He asked if he might have that, and carried it away with him. She had looked into it a thousand times, no doubt; she had done her hair in it; it had reflected her, enclosed her, contained her. He could almost persuade himself that something of her must remain in it. To own it was like owning something of herself. He carried it home with him, hugging it to his side with a kind of passion.

He had prized it, he prized it still, as his dearest treasure, the looking-glass in which her face had been reflected a thousand times; the glass that had contained her, known her; in which something of herself, he felt, must linger. To handle it, look at it, into it, behind it, was like holding a mystic communion with her; it gave him an emotion that was infinitely sweet and bitter, a pain that was dissolved in joy.

The glass lay now, folded in its ivory case, on the chimney-shelf in front of him. That was its place; he always kept it on his chimney-shelf, so that he could see it whenever he glanced round his room. He leaned back in his chair, and looked at it; for a long time his eyes remained fixed upon it. "If she had married me, she would n't have died. My love, my care, would have healed her. She could not have died." Monotonously, automatically, the phrase repeated itself over and over again in his mind, while his eyes remained fixed on the ivory case into which her looking-glass was folded. It was an effect of his fatigue, no doubt, that his eyes, once directed upon an object, were slow to leave it for another; that a phrase once pronounced in his thought had this tendency to repeat itself over and over again.

But at last he roused himself a little, and, leaning forward, put his hand out and up, to take the glass from the shelf. He wished to hold it, to touch it and look into it. As he lifted it towards him, it fell open, the mirror proper being fastened to a leather back, which was glued to the ivory, and formed a hinge. It fell open; and his grasp had been insecure; and the jerk as it opened was enough. It slipped from his fingers, and dropped with a crash upon the hearthstone.

The sound went through him like a physical pain. He sank back in his chair, and closed his eyes. His heart was beating as after a mighty physical exertion. He knew vaguely that a calamity had befallen him; he could vaguely imagine the splinters of shattered glass at his feet. But his physical prostration was so great as to obliterate, to neutralize, emotion. He felt very cold. He felt that he was being hurried along with terrible speed through darkness and cold air. There was the continuous roar of rapid motion in his ears, a faint, dizzy bewilderment in his head. He felt that he was trying to catch hold of things, to stop his progress, but his hands closed upon emptiness; that he was trying to call out for help, but he could make no sound. On — on — on, he was being whirled through some immeasurable abyss of space.

· · · · · · ·

"Ah, yes, he's dead, quite dead," the doctor said. "He has been dead some hours. He must have passed away peacefully, sitting here in his chair."

"Poor gentleman," said the porter's wife. "And a broken looking-glass beside him. Oh, it's a sure sign, a broken looking-glass."

THE REWARD OF VIRTUE.

THE REWARD OF VIRTUE.

He was one of the institutions of the Latin Quarter, one of the least admirable. He haunted the Boulevard St. Michel, hung round the cafés, begged of the passing stranger, picked up cigarette-ends, and would, at a pinch, run errands or do odd jobs.

With his sallow, wrinkled skin, his jungle of gray beard, his thick gray hair, matted and shiny, covering his ears and falling about his shoulders, he was scarcely an attractive-looking person. Besides, he had lost an eye; and its empty socket irresistibly drew your gaze, — an abhorrent vacuum. His clothes would be the odds and ends of students' off-casts, in the last stages of disintegration. He had a chronic stoop; always aimed his surviving eye obliquely at you, from a bent head; and walked with a sort of hangdog shuffle that seemed a general self-denunciation.

Where he slept, whether under a roof or on the pavement, and when, were among his secrets. No matter how late or how early you were abroad, you would be sure to encounter Bibi, wide awake, somewhere in the Boul' Miche, between the Luxembourg and the Rue des Ecoles. That was his beat. Perhaps one of the benches was his home.

He lived in a state of approximate intoxication. I never drew near to him without getting a whiff of alcohol, yet I never saw him radically drunk. His absorbent capacity must have been tremendous. It is certain he spent all the sous he could collect for liquids (he never wasted money upon food; he knew where to go for crusts of bread and broken meat; the back doors of restaurants have their pensioners), and if invited to drink as the guest of another, he would drain tumbler after tumbler continuously, until his entertainer stopped him, and would appear no further over-seas at the end than at the outset. There was something pathetic in his comparative sobriety, like an unfulfilled aspiration.

He was one of the institutions of the Quarter, one of the notabilities. It was a matter of pride (I can't think why) to be on terms of hail-fellowship with him, on terms to thee-and-thou him, and call him by his nickname, Bibi, Bibi Ragoût: a sobriquet that he had come by long before my time, and whose origin I never heard explained. It seemed sufficiently disrespectful, but he accepted it cheerfully, and would often, indeed, employ it in place of the personal pronoun in referring to himself. "You're not going to forget Bibi — you'll not forget poor old Bibi Ragoût?" would be his greeting on the jour de l'an, for instance.

I have said that he would run errands or do odd jobs. The business with which people charged him was not commonly of a nature to throw lustre upon either agent or principal. He would do a student's dirty work, even an étudiante's, in a part of Paris where work to be accounted dirty must needs be very dirty work indeed. The least ignominious service one used to require of him was to act as intermediary with the pawnshop, the clou: a service that he performed to the great satisfaction of his clients, for, what with unbounded impudence and a practice of many years, he knew (as the French slang goes) how to make the nail bleed. We trusted him with our valuables and our money, though it was of record that he had once "done time" for theft. But his victim had been a bourgeois from across the river; we were confident he would deal honorably by a fellow Quaternion — he had the *esprit de corps*.

It was Bibi in his social aspect, however, not in his professional, who especially interested us. It was very much the fashion to ask him to join the company at a café table, to offer him libations, and to "draw" him, — make him talk. He would talk of any subject: of art, literature, politics; of life and morals; of the news of the day. He would regale us with anecdotes of persons, places, events; he had outlasted many generations of students, and had hob-and-nobbed in their grub-period with men who had since become celebrities, as he was now hob-and-nobbing with us. He was quite shameless, quite without reverence for himself or others; his conversation was apt to be highly flavored, scandalous, slanderous, and redundant with ambiguous jests; yet — what made it fascinating and tragical — it was unmistakably the conversation of an educated man. His voice was soft, his accent cultivated, his sentences were nicely chiselled. He knew the *mot juste*, the happy figure, the pat allusion. His touch was light; his address could be almost courtly, so that, on suddenly looking up, you would feel a vague surprise to behold in the speaker, not a polished man of the world in his dress-suit, but this beery old one-eyed vagabond in tatters. It was strange to witness his transitions. At one moment he would be holding high discourse of Goethe, and translating illustrative passages into classic French; at the next, whining about la dèche, and begging for a petite saleté de vingt sous, in the cant of the Paris gutters. Or, from an analysis of the character of some conspicuous personage he had known, he would break into an indecent song, or pass to an interchange of mildewed chaff with Gigolette.

Yes, he was a gentleman. This disreputable old man, whose gray hairs, far from making him venerable, but emphasized his sodden degradation; this tipsy, filthy, obscene old man; this jail-bird, this doer of dirty work, this pander, beggar, outcast, who bore without offence such a title of contempt as Bibi Ragoût, was a fallen gentleman, the wreck of something that had once been noble.

More than the fragmentary outline of his history we did not know. We knew that he was a Russian; that his name was Kasghine; that he had started in life as an officer in the Russian army; that many years ago, for crimes conjectural, he had fled his country; and that long before our day he had already gravitated to where we found him, — the mud of the Boulevard St. Michel.

For crimes conjectural. Some of us believed them to have been political, and fancied that we had in Bibi a specimen of the decayed Nihilist. In view of the fact that he often proclaimed himself a Socialist, this seemed to bear some color of probability; but against it argued the circumstance that of the members of that little clan of Russian refugees which inhabits the southern borderland of the Latin Quarter, not one would have aught to say to Bibi. They gave him the widest of wide berths, and when questioned as to their motives, would only shrug their shoulders, and answer that he was a disgraceful old person, a drunken reprobate, whom, the wonder was not that they avoided, but that any decent people could tolerate. This sounded plausible; still, we felt that if his crimes had been political, they might have regarded him with more indulgence.

Of Bibi himself it was equally futile to inquire. There was one subject on which he would never touch, — his previous condition, his past, before he came to be what we saw. "Yes, I am a gentleman. I am Captain Kasghine. I am a gentleman in allotropic form;" that was as much as I ever heard him say. He enjoyed cloaking himself in mystery, he enjoyed the curiosity it drew upon him; but perhaps he had some remnants of pride, some embers of remorse, some little pain and shame, as well.

Of the other legends afloat, one ran to the effect that he had murdered his wife; a second, that he had poisoned the husband of a lady friend; a third, that he had shown the white feather in battle; a fourth, that he had cheated at cards. Bibi would neither admit nor deny any of these imputations, nor would he manifest the faintest resentment when they were discussed in his presence. He would parry them, smiling complaisantly; and (if it be considered that they were all, as it turned out, abominably false) that seems to show better than anything else to what abysmal depths the man had sunk. Perhaps it shows also, incidentally, how very heartless and unimaginative young people in the Latin Quarter used to be. I have seen Bibi swagger; I have seen him sullen, insolent, sarcastic; I have seen him angry, I have heard him swear: but anything like honestly indignant I never saw him.

I remember one night in the Café de la Source, when Fil de Fer had been treating him to brandy and trying to get him to tell his story; I remember his suddenly turning his one eye in the direction of us men, and launching himself upon a long flight of rhetoric. I can see him still, — his unwashed red hand toying with the stem of his liqueur-glass, or rising from time to time to push his hair from his forehead, over which it dangled in soggy wisps, while, in a dinner-table tone of voice, he uttered these somewhat surprising sentiments.

"You would be horrified, you others, lads of twenty, with your careers before you, — you would be horrified if you thought it possible that you might end your days like Bibi, would you not? You wish to walk a clean path, to prosper, to be respectable, to wear sweet linen, to die honored, regretted. And yet, believe me, we poor devils who fail, who fall, who sink to the bottom, we have our compensation. We see vastly more of the realities of life than those do who succeed and rise to the top. We have an experience that is more essential, more significant. We get the real flavor of life. We sweat in the mire; we drink the lees. But the truth is in the mire; the real flavor is in the lees. Oh, we have our compensation. We wear rags, we eat scraps fit for dogs, we sleep under the arches of bridges. We lie in jails, we are hustled by the police, we are despised by all men. If you offer us drink, and stop to gossip with us for a moment, you only do so to please yourselves with the spectacle of our infamy, our infirmity, our incongruity. We have lost all hope, all self-respect. We are ships that have come to grief, that are foundering, that will presently go down. Yet we are not altogether to be pitied: we know life. To the respectable man, the prosperous, life shows herself only in the world, decently attired: we know her at home in her nudity. For him she has manners, a good behavior, a society smile; with us she is frankly herself, — brutal, if you please, corrupt with disease and vice, sordid, profane, lascivious, but genuine. She is kind to him, but hypocritical, affecting scruples, modesties, pieties, a heart and conscience, attitudinizing, blushing false blushes, weeping crocodile tears; she is cruel to us, but sincere. She is at her ease with us, — unashamed. She shows us her thousand moods. She does n't trouble to keep her secrets from us. She throws off the cloak that hid her foulness, the boot that constrained her cloven hoof. She gives free play to her appetites. We know her.

"Here is the fruit of the tree of life," he went on, extending his open hand. "The respectable man but smells its rind; I eat deep, taste the core. The smell is sweet, perhaps; the taste is deathly bitter. But even so? He that eats of the fruit of the tree of life shares the vision of the gods. He gazes upon the naked face of truth. I don't pretend that the face of truth is beautiful. It is hideous beyond imagination. All hate, all savagery, all evil, glare from it, and all uncleanness is upon it. But it is the face of truth; the sight of it gives an ultimate, a supreme satisfaction."

"Say what you will, at the end of life the important thing is to have lived. Well, when all is over, and the prosperous man and I lie equal in the article of death, our fortunes, conditions, outlooks at last for once the same, our results the same, I shall have lived, I shall have seen, I shall have understood, a thousandfold more than he. I shall have known life in her intimacy; he will have had but a polite acquaintance with her."

The hour for Bibi to put this philosophy to the test was nearer than he suspected. He used to describe himself as "thoroughly cured and seasoned," and to predict that he would "last a good while yet." But, one day in December, a subject of remark in the Boul' Miche was Bibi's absence; and before nightfall the news went abroad that he had been found on the turf, under a tree, in the Avenue de l'Observatoire, dead from a coup de sang, and that he was now lying exposed to the gaze of the curious in the little brick house behind Notre Dame.

A meeting of students was called, at which it was resolved to give Bibi a decent funeral; and in order that his friends who had crossed the river might have an opportunity of assisting at it, a lettre de faire part was published in the newspapers. The Committee who had these matters in charge made an attempt to get a Pope from the Russian Church to officiate; but the holy men were scandalized by the request, and refused it with contumely. So a civil funeral was the best that could be achieved.

On a drizzling, dismal December morning, then, we formed ourselves in a procession of two abreast, and, starting from the Place St. Michel, followed Bibi up his familiar Boulevard to the Cemetery of Montparnasse; and men who would have spurned him yesterday, bared their heads as he passed, and women crossed themselves and muttered prayers. We must have been about a hundred strong, and quite a quarter of our numbers came from beyond the bridges, responsive to our lettre de faire part. A student was told off to march with each visitor; and this arrangement proved the means of my being able to supply the missing chapter of Bibi's story.

The person to whom I found myself assigned was an elderly, military-looking man, with the red rosette in his button-hole; extremely well dressed and groomed; erect, ruddy, bright-eyed; with close-cropped white hair, and a drooping white moustache: the picture of a distinguished, contented, fine old French gentleman, whom I marvelled a good deal to see in this conjunction.

On our way to the graveyard we spoke but little. Our business there over, however, he offered me a seat in his carriage, a brougham that had sauntered after us, for the return. And no sooner was the carriage door closed upon us than he began:—

"I am an old man. I want to talk. Will you listen?

"This death, this funeral, have stirred me deeply. I knew Kasghine years ago in Russia, when we were both young men, he an officer in the Russian army, I an attaché to the French Embassy.

"His career has been a very sad one. It illustrates many sad truths.

"Sometimes — it is trite to say so — an act of baseness, a crime of some sort, may be the beginning, the first cause, of a man's salvation. It pulls him up, wakes his conscience. Aghast at what he has done, he reflects, repents, reforms. That is a comforting circumstance, a token of God's goodness.

"But what shall we say when the exact opposite happens? When it is an act of nobility, of splendid heroism, of magnificent self-devotion, that brings to pass a man's moral downfall? It is horrible to admit such a thing as possible, is it not? And yet, the same man who may be capable of one sudden immense act of heroism, may be quite incapable of keeping up the prolonged, daily, yearly struggle with adversity which that act may entail upon him.

"It was so with Kasghine; it was a very noble action which drove him, an exile, from his country. Thrown upon the streets of Paris, without friends, without money, he had not the stuff in him to stand up against the forces that were in operation to drag him down. Which of us can be sure that he would have that stuff? From begging for work, whereby to earn money, Kasghine fell to begging for money itself. His pride. receiving a thousand wounds, instead of being strengthened by them, was killed. Cleanliness is a luxury, a labor; he began to neglect his person; and, in the case of a gentleman, neglect of the person is generally the first step towards neglect of the spirit. Little by little he lost his civilized character, and reverted to the primitive beast; he was feral.

"But thirty, thirty-five years ago, there were few young men in St. Petersburg with better positions, brighter prospects, than Kasghine's. He belonged to an excellent family; he was intelligent, good-looking, popular; he was a captain in a good regiment. One of his uncles had been minister of war, and stood high in the favor of the Tsar.

"In the spring of 1847, Kasghine's regiment was ordered to Warsaw, and garrisoned in the fortress there. Twenty Polish patriots were confined in the casemates, awaiting execution: men of education, honorable men, men with wives and children, condemned to be hanged because they had conspired together — a foolish, ineffectual conspiracy — against what they regarded as the tyranny of Russia, for the liberty of their country. They had struck no blow, but they had written and talked; and they were to be hanged.

"The fate of these men seemed to Kasghine very unjust, very inhuman. It preyed upon his mind. He took it into his head to rescue them, to contrive their escape. I do not say that this was wise or right; but it was certainly generous. No doubt he had a period of hesitation. On the one hand was his *consigne* as a Russian soldier; on the other, what he conceived to be his duty as a man. He knew that the act he contemplated spelt ruin for himself, that it spelt death; and he had every reason to hold life sweet.

"However, he opened communications with the prisoners in the casemates, and with their friends in the town. And one night he got them all safely out, — by daybreak they were secure in hiding. Kasghine himself remained behind. Some one would have to be punished. If the guilty man fled, an innocent man would be punished.

"Well, he was tried by court-martial, and sentenced to be shot. But the Emperor, out of consideration for Kasghine's family, commuted the sentence to one of hard labor for life in the mines of Kara, — a cruel kindness. After eight years in the mines, with blunted faculties, broken health, disfigured by the loss of an eye, and already no doubt in some measure demoralized by the hardships he had suffered, he was pardoned, — another cruel kindness. He was pardoned on condition that he would leave Russian territory and never enter it again. There are periodic wholesale pardonings, you know, at Kara, to clear the prisons and make rooom for fresh convicts.

"Kasghine's private fortune had been confiscated; his family had ceased all relations with him, and would do nothing for him. He came to Paris, and had to engage in the struggle for existence, — a struggle with which he was totally unfamiliar, for which he was totally unequipped. The only profession he knew was soldiering. He tried to obtain a commission in the French army. International considerations, if no others, put that out of the question. He tried to get work, — teaching, translating. He was not a good teacher; his translations did not please his employers. Remember, his health was enfeebled, he was disfigured by the loss of an eye; he had spent eight years in the mines at Kara. He began to sink. Let those blame him who know how hard it is to swim. From borrowing, from begging, he sank to I dare not guess what. I am afraid there can be no doubt that for a while he served the Russian secret police as a spy; but he proved an unremunerative spy; they turned him off. He took to drink, he sank lower and lower, he became whatever is lowest. I had not seen him or heard of him for years, when, yesterday, I read the announcement of his death in the 'Figaro.'"

The old man set me down at the corner of the Rue Racine. I have never met him again; I have never learned who he was.

The other day, being in Paris, I made a pilgrimage to the Cemetery of Montparnasse, to look at Bibi's grave. The wooden cross we had erected over it was pied with weather-stains, the inscription more than half obliterated, —

ALEXIS DIMITRIEVITCH KASGHINE,

Né à Moscou, le 20 Janvier, 1823,

Mort à Paris, le 20 Décembre, 1884.

Priez pour lui.

A RE-INCARNATION.

A RE-INCARNATION.

WE were, according to our nightly habit, in possession of the Café des Souris, — dear Café des Souris, that is no more ; and our assiduous patronage rumor alleges to have been the death of it, — we were in possession of the Café des Souris, a score or so of us, chiefly English speakers, and all votaries of one or other of the "quatre-z-arts," when the door swung open, and he entered.

Now, the entrance of anybody not a member of our particular cénacle into the Café des Souris, we, who felt (I don't know why) that we had proprietary rights in the establishment, could not help deeming somewhat in the nature of an unwarranted intrusion; so we stopped our talk for an instant, and stared at him, — a man of medium stature, heavily built, with hair that fell to his shoulders, escaping from beneath a broad-brimmed, soft felt hat, knee breeches like a bicyclist's, and, in lieu of overcoat, a sort of doublet, or magnified cape, of buff-colored cloth.

He supported our examination, and the accompanying interval of silence, which ordinary flesh and blood might have found embarrassing, with more than composure, — with, it seemed to me, a dimly perceptible subcutaneous smile, as of satisfaction, — and seated himself at the only vacant table. This world held nothing human worthy to rivet our attention longer than thirty seconds, whence, very soon, we were hot in debate again. It was the first Sunday in May; I need hardly add that our subject-matter was the Vernissage, at which the greater number of us had assisted.

For myself, however, I could not forbid my gaze to wander back from time to time upon the stranger, — an indulgence touching which I felt the less compunction, in that he had (it was a fair inference) got himself up with a deliberate view to attracting just such notice. Else, why the sombrero and knickerbockers, the flowing locks and eccentric yellow cloak? Nay, I think it may have been in part this very note of undisguised vanity in the man that made it difficult to keep one's eyes off him: it tickled the sense of humor, and challenged the curiosity. What would his state of mind be, who, in the dotage of the Nineteenth Century, went laboriously out of his way to cultivate a fragmentary resemblance to — say a spurious Vandyke?

As the heat of the room began to tell upon him, he threw aside his outer garment, and hung up his hat, thereby discovering a velvet jacket and a very low-cut shirt, with unstarched rolling collar, and sailor's knot of pale green Liberty silk. His long hair, of a faded, dusty brown, was brushed straight back from his forehead, and plastered down upon his scalp, in such wise as to lend him a misleading effect of baldness. He wore a drooping brown moustache, and a lustreless brown beard, trimmed to an Elizabethan point. His skin was sallow; his eyes were big, wide apart, of an untransparent buttony brilliancy, and in color dully blue. Taken for all in all, his face, deprived of the adventitious aids of long hair and Elizabethan beard, would have been peculiarly spiritless and insignificant; but from the complacency that shone like an unguent in every line of it, as well as from the studied picturesqueness of his costume, it was manifest that he posed as a unique and interesting character, a being mysterious and romantic, melancholy and rarely gifted, — like the artist in a bad play.

Artist, indeed, of some description, I told myself, he must infallibly be reckoned. What mere professional man or merchant would have the heart to render his person thus conspicuous? And the hypothesis that might have disposed of him as a *model* was excluded by the freshness of his clothes. A poet, painter, sculptor, possibly an actor or musician, — anyhow, something to which the generic name of artist, soiled with all ignoble use, could more or less flatteringly be applied, — I made sure he was; an ornament of our own English-speaking race, moreover, proclaimed such by the light of intelligence that played upon his features as he followed our noisy conversation; and, at a guess, two or three and thirty years of age.

"Anybody know the duffer with the hair?"

This question, started by Charles K. Smith, of Battle Creek, Michigan, U.S.A., and commonly called in the Latin Quarter by his sobriquet of *Chalks*, went our rounds in an undertone; and everybody answered, "No."

"What is it? Can it talk? 'Pears like it can hear and catch on," was Chalks's next remark. "Shall we work the growler on it?"

The process termed by Chalks "working the

growler" was of ancient institution in the Café des Souris; and I believe it is not unknown in other seats of learning, — a custom handed down from generation to generation of students, which, like politeness, costing little, yields generous returns. Should a casual wayfarer, happening amongst us, so far transgress the usages of good society as to volunteer a contribution to our talk, without the preliminary of an introduction, it was the rule instantly to require him to offer the company refreshments; and, I am sorry to have to add, not infrequently, being thirsty, and possessing a lively appreciation of the value of our own money, we would, by a marked affability of bearing, by smiles, nods, glances of sympathetic understanding, or what not, designedly encourage such an one to address us, and so render himself liable to our impost.

"If we don't," continued Chalks, "it will be to fly in the face of Providence. The man is simply bursting to fire his mouth off; he's had something to say swelling in him for the last half-hour. It will be an act of Christian mercy to let him say it. And for myself, I confess I'm rather dry."

Chalks doubtless argued from the eager eye with which the man regarded us; from the uneasy way in which he held his seat, shifting in it, and edging in our direction; and from the tentative manner in which he occasionally coughed.

Now, persuaded by the American, we one by one fell silent, to give our victim his opportunity; whilst those nearest to him baited the trap by looking inquiringly at his face.

It was all he needed.

"I beg your pardon," he began, with no symptom of diffidence, "but I too was at the Vernissage to-day, and some of your comments upon it have surprised me." He spoke with a staccato north-country accent, in a chirpy, querulous little voice; and each syllable seemed to chop the air, like a blow from a small hatchet. "Am I to take it that you are serious when you condemn Bouguereau's great picture as a croûte? 'Croûte,' if I mistake not, is equivalent to the English *daub*?"

Our one-armed waiter, Pierre, had but awaited this crisis to come forward and receive our orders. When they were delivered, Chalks courteously explained the situation to the neophyte, adding that, as a further formality, he must make us acquainted with his name and occupation.

He accepted it in perfectly good part. "I'm sure I shall feel honored if you will drink with me," he said, and settled the reckoning with Pierre.

"Name? Name?" a dozen of us cried, in scattering chorus.

"I had thought that, among so many Englishmen and Americans, some one would have recognized me," he replied. "I am Davis Blake."

He said it as one might say, "I am Mr. Gladstone" — or Lord Salisbury — or Bismarck — with dignity, with an inflection of conscious greatness, it is true, but with neither haughtiness nor ostentation. We, however, are singularly ignorant of contemporary English literature in the Latin Quarter, — our chief reading matter, indeed, being Maupassant and "Le Petit Journal pour Rire;" and though, as we shortly learned, here was a writer whose works were for sale at every bookstall in the United Kingdom, lavishly pirated in the United States, and distributed far and wide by Baron Tauchnitz on the Continent, his announcement left us unenlightened.

"Painter?" demanded Chalks.

A shadow crossed his face. "You are surely familiar with my name?"

"Never heard it that I know of," answered Chalks; then, raising his voice, "Any gentleman present ever heard of — what did you say your name was?" he asked in an aside; and, being informed, went on, "of Mr. Davis Blake?"

No one spoke.

"Mud?" queried Chalks.

"Mud?" repeated Mr. Blake, perplexed.

"He means to inquire whether you are a sculptor," ventured I.

"A sculptor, — certainly not." He spoke sharply. throwing back his head. "It is impossible that no one here should have heard of me; and this pretence of ignorance is meant as a practical joke. I am a novelist, — one of the best-known novelists living. I am Davis Blake, the author of 'Crispin Dorr,' and 'The Card-Dealer.' My portrait, with a short biographical sketch, appeared in the 'Illustrated Gazette' not a month ago. My works have been translated into French, German, Russian, and Italian. Of 'The Card-Dealer,' upwards of thirty thousand copies have been sold in Great Britain alone."

"Ah, then you could well afford to stand us drinks," was Chalks's cheerful commentary. "We ain't much on book-learning, this side the river, Mr. Blake. We're plain, blunt men, that ain't ashamed of manual labor, — horny-handed sons of toil, in short. But we're proud to meet a cultivated gentleman like yourself, all the same, and can appreciate him when met."

Blake laughed rather lamely, and responded, "I perceive that you are a humorist. Your countrymen are great admirers of my writings; of 'Crispin Dorr,' I am told, there are no fewer than three rival editions in the market; and I have received complimentary letters and requests for my autograph, from all parts of the United States. I think that the quality of American humor has been overrated; but I can forgive a jest at my own expense, provided it be not meant in malice."

"Every novice in our order, sir," said Chalks, "must approve his mettle by undergoing something in the nature of an initiatory ordeal. We may now drop foolery, and converse like intelligent human beings. You were asking our opinion of Willy's daub — "

"Willy?" questioned Blake.

"Ay — Bouguereau. Isn't his front name William?" And Chalks, speaking as it were ex cathedra, made very short work indeed of Monsieur Bouguereau's claims to rank as a painter. Blake listened with open-eyed wonder. But we are difficult critics, we of the Paris art schools, between the ages of twenty and twenty-five; cold, cynical, suspicious as any Old Bailey judge; and rare is the man whose work can sustain our notice, and get off with lighter censure than "croûte" or "plat d'épinards." We grow more lenient, however, as we advance in years. Already, at thirty, we begin to detect signs of promise in other canvases than our own. At forty, conceivably, we shall even admit a certain degree of actual merit.

By and by Chalks, having concluded his pronouncement, and drifted to another corner of the room, Blake and I fell into separate talk.

"I must count it a piece of exceptional good fortune," he informed me, "to have made the acquaintance of your little coterie this evening. I am on the point of writing a novel, in which it will be necessary that my hero should pass several years as a student in the Latin Quarter; and I have run over from London for the especial purpose of collecting local color. No doubt you will be able to help me with a hint or two as to the best mode of setting about it."

"I can think of none better than to come here and live for a while," said I.

"I only arrived last night, and I put up at the Grand Hotel. But it was quite my intention to move across the river directly I could find suitable lodgings. Do you know of any that you could recommend?"

"If you want to see student life par excellence, you can scarcely improve upon the shop I'm in myself,— the Hôtel du Saint-Esprit, in the Rue St. Jacques."

And after he had examined me in some detail touching that house of entertainment, "Yes," he said, "then, if you will bespeak a room for me there, I'll come to-morrow and stop for a week or ten days."

"A week or ten days?" I questioned.

"I can't spare more than a fortnight. I must be back in town by the 20th."

"But what can you hope to learn of Latin Quarter customs in a fortnight? One ought to live here for a year, at the very least, before attempting to write us up."

"Ah," he rejoined, shaking his head and gazing dreamily at something invisible beyond the smoky atmosphere of the café, "a man with dramatic insight can learn as much in a fortnight as an ordinary person in half a lifetime. Intuition and inspiration take the place of the note-book and the yard-stick. The author of 'The Merchant of Venice' had never visited Italy. In 'Crispin Dorr' I have described a tempest and a shipwreck at which old sailors shudder; and my longest voyage has been from Holyhead to Kingstown. Besides," he added, with a bow and smile, "for the Latin Quarter, if you will take me under your protection, I shall, I am sure, benefit by the services of a capital cicerone."

And the next afternoon he arrived. I met him at the threshold of the hotel, introduced him to our landlady, Madame Pamparagoux (who stared rather wildly, not being accustomed to see her lodgers so mediævally attired), and showed him upstairs to the room I had engaged.

There he invited me to be seated while he unpacked his portmanteau and put his things in order. These, I noticed, were un-Britishly few and simple. I could discern no vestiges of either sponge or tub. As he moved backwards and forwards between his chest of drawers and dressing-table, he would cast frequent affectionate glances at his double, now in the glass of the armoire, now in that above the chimney. He was favoring me meantime with a running monologue of an autobiographical complexion.

"I am a self-educated man. My father was a wine merchant in Leeds. At sixteen he put me to serve in the shop of a cousin, a print-seller. It was there,

I think, that my literary instincts awoke. I contributed occasional art notes to a local paper. At twenty I came up to London and began my definite career, as a reporter. I was soon earning thirty shillings a week, which seemed to me magnificent. But I aspired to higher things. I felt within me the stirrings of what I could not help believing to be genius, — true genius. I longed to distinguish myself, to emerge from the crowd, from the background, to make myself remarked, to do something, to be somebody, to see my name a famous one. I was fortunate enough at this epoch to attract the notice of X———, the poet. He believed in me, and encouraged me to believe in myself. It is one of the regrets of my life that he died before I had achieved my celebrity. However, I have achieved it. My name is a household word wherever the English language is read. I have written the only novels of my time that are sure to live. They will live, not only by virtue of their style and matter, but because of a quality they possess which I must call *universal*, — a quality which appeals with equal force to readers of every rank, and which will procure for them as wide a popularity five hundred years hence as they enjoy to-day. I call them novels, but they are really prose-poems. The novel," he continued, rising for an instant to impersonal heights, "the novel is the literary form or expression of my period, as the drama was that of Shakespeare's, the epic of Homer's. Do you follow me ? Ah, here is a copy of 'Crispin Dorr'— here is 'The Card-Dealer.' Take them and read them, and return them when you have finished. Being author's copies, they possess an exceptional value. This is my autograph upon the fly-leaf. This is a photograph of my wife. She is a good woman, but has no great literary culture, and we are not so happy together as I could wish. Men of commanding parts seldom make good husbands, and I committed the imprudence of marrying very young. My wife, you see, belongs to that class of society from which I have risen. I am the son of a wine merchant, yet I dine with peers, and have been favored with smiles from peeresses. My wife has not kept pace with me. This is my little girl, — our only child, — my daughter Judith. Here is the 'Illustrated Gazette,' with the portrait of myself."

Some of us in the Latin Quarter found the man's egotism insupportable, and gave him a wide berth. Others, more numerous, among them the irrepressible Chalks, made it an object of derision, and would exhaust their ingenuity in efforts to lead him on, and entice him into more and more egregious exhibitions of it; while, if they did not laugh in his face, they took, at least, no slightest pains to conceal their jubilant interchange of winks and nudges.

"If he were only an ass," Chalks urged, "one might feel disposed to spare him. A merciful man is merciful to a beast. But he's such a cad, to boot, — bandying his wife's name about the Latin Quarter, telling Tom, Dick, and Harry of their conjugal differences, and boasting of his successes with other women!"

A few of us, however, could not prevent an element of pity from tincturing our amusement. If his self-conceit was comical, by reason of its candor, it was surely pitiable, because of the poor dwarfed starveling of a soul that it revealed. Here was a man, with life in his veins, and round about him the whole mystery and richness of creation, — and he could seriously think of nothing save how, by his dress, by his speech, his postures, to render himself the observed of all observers!

Wherever he went, in whatever company he found himself, that was the sole thing he cared for, — to be the centre of attention, to be looked at, listened to, recognized and admired as a celebrity. And if the event happened otherwise, if he had ground for the suspicion that the people near him were suffering their minds to wander to another topic, his face would darken, his attitude become distinctly one of rancor. With Chalks, familiarity bred boldness; he made the latter days of Blake's sojourn amongst us exceedingly unhappy.

"Now, Mr. Blake," he would say, "we are going to talk of art and love and things in general for a while, to rest our brains from the author of 'Crispin Dorr.' Please step into the corner there and sulk."

And he had a bit of slang, which he set to a bar of music, and would sing, as if in absence of mind, whenever the conversation lapsed, to the infinite annoyance of Mr. Blake: —

"Git your hair cut — git your hair cut — git your hair cut — *short!*"

"If that is meant for me," Blake once protested, "I take it as discourteous in the last degree."

"My dear sir, you were twenty thousand leagues from my thoughts. And as for getting your hair cut, I beseech you, don't. You would shear away the fabric of our joy," Chalks answered.

Blake had a curiously exaggerated notion of his fame; and his jealousy thereof surpassed the jealousy of women. He took it for granted that everybody had heard of him, and bridled, as at a personal affront, when he met any one who hadn't. If you fell into chance talk with him, in ignorance of his identity, he could not let three minutes pass without informing you. And then, if you appeared not adequately impressed, he would wax ill-tempered. He was genuinely convinced that his person and his actions were affairs of consuming interest to all the world. To be something, to do something, perhaps he honestly aspired; but to *seem* something was certainly his ruling passion.

One Sunday afternoon, at his suggestion, we went together to the studio of Z————, and I introduced him to the Master. But, as we moved about the vast room, among those small, priceless canvases, the consciousness grew upon me that my companion was in some distress of mind. His eye wandered; his utterances were brief and dry. At length he got me into a corner, and remarked, "You introduced me simply as Mr. Blake. He evidently doesn't realize who I am."

"Oh, these Frenchmen are so indifferent to things not French, you know," said I.

"Yes — but — still — I wish you could make an occasion to let him know. In introducing me you might have added 'a distinguished English author.'"

"But do you quite realize who *he* is?" I cried. "He's jolly near the most distinguished living painter."

"Never mind. He is treating me now as he might Brown, Jones, or Robinson." As this was with a superfine consideration, it seemed unreasonable to demand a difference. Nevertheless, I seized an opportunity to whisper in the Master's ear a word or two to the desired effect. "Tiens!" he returned, composedly, and continued to treat his visitor precisely as he had done from the beginning.

Blake had announced that he wanted to gather information about the Latin Quarter, and I don't doubt that his purpose was sincere; but he employed a novel method of attaining it. We took him everywhere, we showed him everything; I could never observe that he either looked or listened. He would sit (or stand or walk), his eye craving admiration from our faces; his tongue wagging about himself; his early hardships, his first success, his habits of work, his troubles with his wife, his liaison with Lady Blank, his tastes in fruits and wines, his handwriting, his very teeth and boots. He passed his life in a sort of trance, an ecstasy of self-absorption; he had fallen in love with his own conception of himself, like a metaphysical Narcissus. This idiosyncrasy was the means of defeating various conspiracies, in which Chalks, of course, was the prime mover, calculated to impose upon his credulity, and send him back to London loaded down with misinformation.

"His cheek, by Christopher!" cried Chalks. "Live in the Quarter for a fortnight, keep his eyes and ears shut, talk perpetually of Davis Blake, and read nothing but his own works, and then go home and write a book about it. I'll quarter him!"

But Chalks counted without his man. That Monsieur Bullier, the founder of the Closerie des Lilas, was also Professor of Moral Philosophy in the Collège de France; that the word "étudiante"(for Blake had only a tourist's smattering of French) should literally be translated *student*, and that the young ladies who bore it as a name were indeed pursuing rigorous courses of study at the Sorbonne; that it was obligatory upon a freshman (nouveau) in the Quarter to shave his head and wear wooden shoes for the first month after his matriculation, — from these and kindred superstitions Blake was saved by his grand talent for never paying attention.

In the mean while some of us had read his books: chromo-lithographs, struck in the primary colors; pasteboard complications of passion and adventure, with the conservative entanglement of threadbare marionnettes — a hero, tall, with golden brown moustaches and blue eyes; a heroine, lissome, with "sunny locks;" then a swarthy villain, for the most part a nobleman, and his Spanish-looking female accomplice, who had an uncomfortable habit of delivering her remarks "from between clenched teeth," and, generally, "in a blood-chilling hiss," — the narrative set forth in a sustained *fortissimo*, and punctuated by the timely exits of the god from the machine. Never a felicity, never an impression. I fancy he had made his notes of human nature whilst observing the personages of a melodrama at a provincial theatre. He loved the obvious sentiment, the obvious and but approximate word.

But the climax of his infatuation was not disclosed till the night before he left us. Again we were in session at the Café des Souris, and the talk had turned upon metempsychosis. Blake, for a wonder, pricked up his ears and appeared to listen, at the same time watching his chance to take the floor. Half-a-dozen men had their say first, however; then he cut in.

"Metempsychosis is not a theory, it is a fact. I can testify to it from my personal experience. I know it. I can distinctly recall my former life. I can tell you who I was, who my friends were, what I did, what I felt, everything, down to the very dishes I preferred for dinner."

Chalks scanned Blake's features for an instant with an intentness that suggested a mingling of perplexity and malice; then, all at once, I saw a light flash in his eyes, which forthwith began to twinkle in a manner that struck me as ominous.

"In my early youth," Blake continued, "this memory of mine was, if I may so phrase it, piecemeal and occasional. Feeling that I was no ordinary man, conscious of strange forces struggling in me, I would obtain, as it were, glimpses, fleeting and unsatisfactory, into a former state. Then they would go, not for long intervals to return. As time elapsed, however, these glimpses, to call them so, became more frequent and lasting, the intervals of oblivion shorter; and at last, one day on Hampstead Heath, I identified myself in a sudden burst of insight. I was walking on the Heath, and thinking of my work,—marvelling at a certain quality I had discerned in it, which, I was convinced, would assure it everlasting life: a quality that seemed not unfamiliar to me, and yet which I could associate with none of the writers whose names passed in review before my mind; not with Byron, or Shelley, or Keats, not with Wordsworth or Coleridge, Goethe or Dante, not even with Homer. I mean the quality which I call *universal*,— universal in its authenticity, universal in its appeal. By and by, I took out a little pocket mirror that I always carry, and looked into it, studying my face. One glance sufficed. There, suddenly, on Hampstead Heath, the whole thing flashed upon me. I saw, I understood; I realized who I was, I remembered everything."

"Stop right there, Mr. Blake," called out Chalks, in stentorian tones. "Don't you say another word. I'm going to hail you by your right name in half-a-minute. I guess I must have recognized you the very first time I clapped eyes on your distinguished physiognomy; only I couldn't just *place* you, as we say over in America. But there was a je ne sais quoi in the whole cut of your jib as familiar to me as rolls and coffee. I tried and tried to think when and where I'd had the pleasure before. But now that you speak of a former state of existence, — why, I'm *there!* It was all I needed, just a little hint like that, to jog my memory. Talk about entertaining angels unawares! The beard, eh? And the yaller cloak? And ain't there a statue of you up Boulevard Haussmann way? Shakesy, old man, shake!"

And Chalks got hold of his victim's hand and wrung it fervently. "I'm particularly glad to meet you this way," he added, "because I was Queen Elizabeth myself; and I can't begin to tell you how sort of out of it I felt, alone here with all this degenerate posterity."

Blake coldly withdrew his hand, frowning loftily at Chalks. "You should reserve your nonsense for more appropriate occasions," he said. "Though you speak in a spirit of foolish levity, you have builded better than you knew. I am indeed Shakespeare reincarnated. My books alone would prove it; they could have been dictated by no other mind. But — look at this."

He produced from an interior pocket, a case of red morocco and handed it to me. "*You*," he said, with a flattering emphasis upon the pronoun, "you are a man who can treat a serious matter seriously. What do you think of that?"

The case contained a photograph, and the photograph represented the head and shoulders of Mr. Blake and a bust of Shakespeare, placed cheek by jowl. In the pointed beard and the wide-set eyes there were, perhaps, the rudiments of something remotely like a likeness.

"Is n't that conclusive?" he demanded. "Does n't that place the fact beyond the reach of question?"

"You 've got more hair than you used to have," said Chalks. "I 'm talking of the front hair, — your forehead ain't as high as it was. But your back hair is all right enough."

"You have put your finger on the one, the only, point of difference," assented Blake.

On our way home he took my arm, and pitched his voice in the key of confidence. "I am writing my autobiography, from my birth in Stratford down to the present day. It will be in two parts; the interim when people thought me dead, marking their separation. I was not dead; I slept a dreamless sleep. Presently I shall sleep again, — as men say, die; then doubtless wake again. Life and death are but sleeping and waking on a larger scale. Our little life is rounded with a sleep. It is the swing of the pendulum, the revolution of the orb. Yes, I am writing my autobiography. So little is known of the private history of Shakespeare, conceive the boon it will be to mankind. I shall leave the manuscripts to my executors, for them to publish after I have lain down to my next long rest. Of special value will be the chapters telling how I wrote the plays, settling disputed readings, closing all controversy upon the sanity of Hamlet, and divulging the true personality of Mr. W. H."

He came into my room for a little visit before going to bed. There, candle in hand, he gazed long and earnestly into my chimney-glass.

"Yes," he sighed at last, "it is solely in the quantity of my hair that the resemblance fails."

I understood now why he trained it back and plastered it down over his scalp, as he did; at a rough glance, you might have got the impression that the crown of his head was bald. I suppose he is the only man in two hemispheres who finds the opposite condition a matter of regret.

FLOWER O' THE QUINCE.

FLOWER O' THE QUINCE.

I

THEODORE VELLAN had been out of England for more than thirty years. Thirty odd years ago the set he lived in had been startled and mystified by his sudden flight and disappearance. At that time his position here had seemed a singularly pleasant one. He was young, — he was seven or eight and twenty; he was fairly well off, — he had something like three thousand a year, indeed; he belonged to an excellent family, — the Shropshire Vellans, of whom the titled head, Lord Vellan of Norshingfield, was his uncle; he was good-looking, amiable, amusing, popular; and he had just won a seat in the House of Commons (as junior member for Sheffingham), where, since he was believed to be ambitious as well as clever, it was generally expected that he would go far.

Then, quite suddenly, he had applied for the Chiltern Hundreds, and left England. His motives for this unlikely course he explained to no one. To a few intimate friends he wrote brief letters of farewell. "I am off for a journey round the world. I shall be gone an indefinite time." The indefinite time ended by defining itself as upwards of thirty years, for the first twenty of which only his solicitor and his bankers could have given you his address, and they wouldn't. For the last ten he was understood to be living in the island of Porto Rico, and planting sugar. Meanwhile his uncle had died, and his cousin (his uncle's only son) had succeeded to the peerage. But the other day his cousin, too, had died, and died childless, so that the estates and dignities had devolved upon himself. With that a return to England became an obligation; there were a score of minor beneficiaries under his cousin's will, whose legacies could not, without great delay, be paid unless the new lord was at hand.

II

Mrs. Sandryl-Kempton sat before the fire in her wide, airy, faded drawing-room, and thought of the Theodore Vellan of old days, and wondered what the present Lord Vellan would be like. She had got a note from him that morning, despatched from Southampton the day before, announcing, "I shall be in town to-morrow, at Bowden's Hotel, in Cork Street," and asking when he might come to her. She had answered by telegraph, "Come and dine at eight to-night," to which he had wired back an acceptance. Thereupon, she had told her son that he must dine at his club; and now she was seated before her fire, waiting for Theodore Vellan to arrive, and thinking of thirty years ago.

She was a bride then, and her husband, her brother Paul, and Theodore Vellan were bound in a league of ardent young-mannish friendship,—a friendship that dated from the time when they had been undergraduates together at Oxford. She thought of the three handsome, happy, highly endowed young men, and of the brilliant future she had foreseen for each of them, — her husband at the Bar, her brother in the Church, and Vellan — not in politics, she could never understand his political aspirations, they seemed quite at odds with the rest of his character, — but in literature, as a poet, for he wrote verse which she considered very unusual and pleasing. She thought of this, and then she remembered that her husband was dead, that her brother was dead, and that Theodore Vellan had been dead to his world, at all events, for thirty years. Not one of them had in any way distinguished himself; not one had in any measure fulfilled the promise of his youth.

Her memories were sweet and bitter; they made her heart glow and ache. Vellan, as she recalled him, had been, before all things, gentle. He was witty, he had humor, he had imagination; but he was, before all things, gentle, — with the gentlest voice, the gentlest eyes, the gentlest manners. His gentleness, she told herself, was the chief element of his charm, — his gentleness, which was really a phase of his modesty. "He was very gentle, he was very modest, he was very graceful and kind," she said; and she remembered a hundred instances of his gentleness, his modesty, his kindness. Oh, but he was no milksop. He had plenty of spirit, plenty of fun; he was boyish, he could romp. And at that, a scene repeated itself to her mind, — a scene that had passed in this same drawing-room more than thirty years ago. It was tea-time, and on the tea-table lay a dish of pearl biscuits, and she and her husband and Vellan were alone. Her husband took a handful of pearl biscuits, and tossed them one by one into the air, while Vellan threw back his head, and caught them in his mouth as they came down,—that was one of his accomplishments. She smiled as she remembered it, but at the same time she put her handkerchief to her eyes.

"Why did he go away? What could it have been?" she wondered, her old bewilderment at his conduct, her old longing to comprehend it, reviving with something of the old force. "Could it have been . . .? Could it have been . . .?" And an old guess, an old theory, one she had never spoken to anybody, but had pondered much in silence, again presented itself interrogatively to her mind.

The door opened; the butler mumbled a name; and she saw a tall, white-haired, pale old man smiling at her and holding out his hands. It took her a little while to realize who it was. With an unthinking disallowance for the action of time, she had been expecting a young fellow of eight and twenty, brown-haired and ruddy.

Perhaps he, on his side, was taken aback a little to meet a middle-aged lady in a cap.

III

After dinner he would not let her leave him, but returned with her to the drawing-room, and she said that he might smoke. He smoked odd little Cuban cigarettes, whereof the odor was delicate and aromatic. They had talked of everything; they had laughed and sighed over their ancient joys and sorrows. We know how, in the Courts of Memory, Mirth and Melancholy wander hand in hand. She had cried a little when her husband and her brother were first spoken of, but at some comic reminiscence of them, a moment afterwards, she was smiling through her tears. "Do you remember so-and-so?" and "What has become of such-a-one?" were types of the questions they asked each other, conjuring up old friends and enemies like ghosts out of the past. Incidentally, he had described Porto Rico and its negroes and its Spaniards, its climate, its fauna, and its flora.

In the drawing-room they sat on opposite sides of the fire, and were silent for a bit. Profiting by the permission she had given him, he produced one of his Cuban cigarettes, opened it at its ends, unrolled it, rolled it up again, and lit it.

"Now the time has come for you to tell me what I most want to know," she said.

"What is that?"

"Why you went away."

"Oh," he murmured.

She waited a minute. Then, "Tell me," she urged.

"Do you remember Mary Isona?" he asked.

She glanced up at him suddenly, as if startled. "Mary Isona? Yes, of course."

"Well, I was in love with her."

"You were in love with Mary Isona?"

"I was very much in love with her. I have never got over it, I'm afraid."

She gazed fixedly at the fire. Her lips were compressed. She saw a slender girl in a plain black frock, with a sensitive pale face, luminous, sad dark eyes, and a mass of dark waving hair, — Mary Isona, of Italian parentage, a little music-teacher, whose only relation to the world Theodore Vellan lived in was professional. She came into it for an hour or two at a time now and then, to play or to give a music-lesson.

"Yes," he repeated, "I was in love with her. I have never been in love with any other woman. It seems ridiculous for an old man to say it, but I am in love with her still. An old man? Are we ever really old? Our body grows old, our skin wrinkles, our hair turns white; but the mind, the spirit, the heart? The thing we call "I"? Anyhow, not a day, not an hour, passes, but I think of her, I long for her, I mourn for her. You knew her — you knew what she was. Do you remember her playing? her wonderful eyes? her beautiful pale face? And how the hair grew round her forehead? And her talk, her voice, her intelligence! Her taste, her instinct, in literature, in art, — it was the finest I have ever met."

"Yes, yes, yes," Mrs. Kempton said slowly. "She was a rare woman. I knew her intimately, — better than any one else, I think. I knew all the unhappy circumstances of her life, — her horrid, vulgar mother; her poor, dreamy, inefficient father; her poverty; how hard she had to work. You were in love with her. Why didn't you marry her?"

"My love was not returned."

"Did you ask her?"

"No. It was needless; it went without saying."

"You never can tell. You ought to have asked her."

"It was on the tip of my tongue, of course, to do so a hundred times. My life was passed in torturing myself with the question whether I had any chance, in hoping and fearing. But as often as I found myself alone with her, I knew it was hopeless. Her manner to me, — it was one of frank friendliness. There was no mistaking it. She never thought of loving me."

"You were wrong not to ask her. One never can be sure. Oh! why didn't you ask her?" His old friend spoke with great feeling.

He looked at her, surprised and eager. "Do you really think she might have cared for me?"

"Oh, you ought to have told her; you ought to have asked her," she repeated.

"Well — now you know why I went away."

"Yes."

"When I heard of her — her — death" — he could not bring himself to say her suicide — "there was nothing else for me to do. It was so hideous, so unutterable. To go on with my old life, in the old place, among the old people, was quite impossible. I wanted to follow her, to do what she had done. The only alternative was to fly as far from England, as far from myself, as I could."

"Sometimes" Mrs. Kempton confessed by and by, "sometimes I wondered whether, possibly, your disappearance could have had any such connection with Mary's death, — it followed it so immediately. I wondered sometimes whether, perhaps, you had cared for her. But I couldn't believe it; it was only because the two things happened one upon the other. Oh, why didn't you tell her? It is dreadful, dreadful!"

IV

When he had left her, she sat still for a little while before the fire.

"Life is a chance to make mistakes, — a chance to make mistakes. Life is a chance to make mistakes."

It was a phrase she had met in a book she was reading the other day: then she had smiled at it; now it rang in her ears like the voice of a mocking demon.

"Yes, a chance to make mistakes," she said, half aloud.

She rose and went to her desk, unlocked a drawer, turned over its contents, and took out a letter, — an old letter, for the paper was yellow, and the ink was faded. She came back to the fireside, and unfolded the letter and read it. It covered six pages of notepaper, in a small feminine hand; it was a letter Mary Isona had written to her, Margaret Kempton, the night before she died, more than thirty years ago. The writer recounted the many harsh circumstances of her life; but they would all have been bearable, she said, save for one great and terrible secret. She had fallen in love with a man who was scarcely conscious of her existence; she, a little obscure Italian music-teacher, had fallen in love with Theodore Vellan. It was as if she had fallen in love with an inhabitant of another planet, the worlds they respectively belonged to were so far apart. She loved him — she loved him — and she knew her love was hopeless, and she could not bear it. Oh, yes; she met him sometimes, here and there, at houses she went to to play, to give lessons. He was civil to her; he was more than civil, — he was kind; he talked to her about literature and music. "He is so gentle, so strong, so wise; but he has never thought of me as a woman, — a woman who could love, who could be loved. Why should he? If the moth falls in love with the star, the moth must suffer. . . . I am cowardly; I am weak; I am what you will; but I have more than I can bear. Life is too hard, — too hard. To-morrow I shall be dead. You will be the only person to know why I died, and you will keep my secret."

"Oh, the pity of it — the pity of it!" murmured Mrs. Kempton. "I wonder whether I ought to have shown him Mary's letter."

WHEN I AM KING.

WHEN I AM KING.

" Qu'y faire, mon Dieu, qu'y faire? "

I HAD wandered into a tangle of slummy streets, and began to think it time to inquire my way back to the hotel; then, turning a corner, I came out upon the quays. At one hand there was the open night, with the dim forms of many ships, and stars hanging in a web of masts and cordage; at the other, the garish illumination of a row of public-houses: Au Bonheur du Matelot, Café de la Marine, Brasserie des Quatre Vents, and so forth, — rowdy-looking shops enough, designed for the entertainment of the forecastle. But they seemed to promise something in the nature of local color; and I entered the Brasserie des Quatre Vents.

It proved to be a brasserie-à-femmes; you were waited upon by ladies, lavishly rouged and in regardless toilets, who would sit with you and chat, and partake of refreshments at your expense. The front part of the room was filled up with tables, where half a hundred customers, talking at the top of their voices, raised a horrid din, — sailors, soldiers, a few who might be clerks or tradesmen, and an occasional workman in his blouse. Beyond, there was a cleared space, reserved for dancing, occupied by a dozen couples, clumsily toeing it; and on a platform, at the far end, a man pounded a piano. All this in an atmosphere hot as a furnace-blast, and poisonous with the fumes of gas, the smells of bad tobacco, of musk, alcohol, and humanity.

The musician faced away from the company, so that only his shoulders and the back of his gray head were visible, bent over his keyboard. It was sad to see a gray head in that situation; and one wondered what had brought it there, what story of vice or weakness or evil fortune. Though his instrument was harsh, and he had to bang it violently to be heard above the roar of conversation, the man played with a kind of cleverness, and with certain fugitive suggestions of good style. He had once studied an art, and had hopes and aspirations, who now, in his age, was come to serve the revels of a set of drunken sailors, in a disreputable tavern, where they danced with prostitutes. I don't know why, but from the first he drew my attention; and I left my handmaid to count her charms neglected, while I sat and watched him, speculating about him in a melancholy way, with a sort of vicarious shame.

But presently something happened to make me forget him, — something of his own doing. A dance had ended, and after a breathing spell he began to play an interlude. It was an instance of how tunes, like perfumes, have the power to wake sleeping memories. The tune he was playing now, simple and dreamy like a lullaby, and strangely at variance with the surroundings, whisked me off in a twinkling, far from the actual — ten, fifteen years backwards — to my student life in Paris, and set me to thinking, as I had not thought for many a long day, of my hero, friend, and comrade, Edmund Pair; for it was a tune of Pair's composition, a melody he had written to a nursery rhyme, and used to sing a good deal, half in fun, half in earnest, to his lady-love, Godelinette:

> "Lavender's blue, diddle-diddle,
> Lavender's green;
> When I am king, diddle-diddle,
> You shall be queen."

It is certain he meant very seriously that if he ever came into his kingdom, Godelinette should be queen. The song had been printed, but, so far as I knew, had never had much vogue; and it seemed an odd chance that this evening, in a French seaport town where I was passing a single night, I should stray by hazard into a sailors' pothouse and hear it again.

Edmund Pair lived in the Latin Quarter when I did, but he was no longer a mere student. He had published a good many songs; articles had been written about them in the newspapers; and at his rooms you would meet the men who had "arrived," — actors, painters, musicians, authors, and now and then a politician, — who thus recognized him as more or less one of themselves. Everybody liked him; everybody said, "He is splendidly gifted; he will go far." A few of us already addressed him, half-playfully perhaps, as cher maître.

He was three or four years older than I, — eight- or nine-and-twenty to my twenty-five, — and I was still in the schools; but for all that we were great chums. Quite apart from his special talent, he was a remarkable man, — amusing in talk, good-looking, generous, affectionate. He had read; he had travelled; he had hob-and-nobbed with all sorts and conditions of people.

He had wit, imagination, humor, and a voice that made whatever he said a cordial to the ear. For myself, I admired him, enjoyed him, loved him, with equal fervor; he had all of my hero-worship, and the lion's share of my friendship; perhaps I was vain as well as glad to be distinguished by his intimacy. We used to spend two or three evenings a week together, at his place or at mine, or over the table of a café, talking till the small hours, — Elysian sessions, at which we smoked more cigarettes and emptied more bocks than I should care to count. On Sundays and holidays we would take long walks arm-in-arm in the Bois, or, accompanied by Godelinette, go to Viroflay or Fontainebleau, lunch in the open, bedeck our hats with wild-flowers, and romp like children. He was tall and slender, with dark, waving hair, a delicate aquiline profile, a clear brown skin, and gray eyes, alert, intelligent, kindly. I fancy the Boulevard St. Michel, flooded with sunshine, broken here and there by long crisp shadows; trams and omnibuses toiling up the hill, tooting their horns; students and étudiantes sauntering gayly backwards and forwards on the trottoir; an odor of asphalte, of caporal tobacco; myself one of the multitude on the terrace of a café; and Edmund and Godelinette coming to join me, — he with his swinging stride, a gesture of salutation, a laughing face; she in the freshest of bright-colored spring toilets: I fancy this, and it seems an adventure of the golden age. Then we would drink our apéritifs, our Turin bitter, perhaps our absinthe, and go off to dine together in the garden at Lavenue's.

Godelinette was a child of the people, but Pair had

done wonders by way of civilizing her. She had learned English, and prattled it with an accent so quaint and sprightly as to give point to her otherwise perhaps somewhat commonplace observations. She was fond of reading; she could play a little; she was an excellent housewife, and generally a very good-natured and quite presentable little person. She was Parisian and adaptable. To meet her, you would never have suspected her origin; you would have found it hard to believe that she had been the wife of a drunken tailor, who used to beat her. One January night, four or five years before, Pair had surprised this gentleman publicly pummelling her in the Rue Gay-Lussac. He hastened to remonstrate; and the husband went off, hiccoughing of his outraged rights, and calling the universe to witness that he would have the law of the meddling stranger. Pair picked the girl up (she was scarcely eighteen then, and had only been married a six-month), — he picked her up from where she had fallen, half fainting, on the pavement, carried her to his lodgings, which were at hand, and sent for a doctor. In his manuscript-littered study, for rather more than nine weeks, she lay on a bed of fever, the consequence of blows, exhaustion, and exposure. When she got well there was no talk of her leaving. Pair could n't let her go back to her tailor; he could n't turn her into the streets. Besides, during the months that he had nursed her, he had somehow conceived a great tenderness for her; it made his heart burn with grief and anger to think of what she suffered in the past, and he yearned to sustain and protect and comfort her for the future. This perhaps was no more than natural; but, what rather upset the calculations of his friends, she, towards whom he had established himself in the relation of a benefactor, bore him, instead of a grudge therefor, a passionate gratitude and affection. So, Pair said, they were only waiting till her tailor should drink himself to death, to get married; and meanwhile, he exacted for her all the respect that would have been due to his wife; and everybody called her by his name. She was a pretty little thing, very daintily formed, with tiny hands and feet, and big gipsyish brown eyes; and very delicate, very fragile, — she looked as if anything might carry her off. Her name, Godeleine, seeming much too grand and mediæval for so small and actual a person, Pair had turned it into Godelinette.

We all said, "He is splendidly gifted; he will do great things." He had studied at Cambridge and at Leipsic before coming to Paris. He was learned, enlightened, and extremely modern; he was a hard worker. We said he would do great things; but I thought in those days, and indeed I still think — and, what is more to the purpose, men who were themselves musicians and composers, men whose names are known, were before me in thinking — that he had already done great things, that the songs he had already published were achievements. They seemed to us original in conception, accomplished and felicitous in treatment; they were full of melody and movement, full of harmonic surprises; they had style and they had "go." One would have imagined they must please at once the cultivated and the general public. I could never understand why they were n't popular. They would be printed; they would be praised at length, and under distinguished signatures, in the reviews; they would enjoy an unusual success of approbation; but — they would n't *sell*, and they would n't get themselves sung at concerts. If they had been too good, if they had been over the heads of people — but they were n't. Plenty of work quite as good, quite as modern, yet no whit more tuneful or interesting, was making its authors rich. We could n't understand it; we had to conclude it was a fluke, a question of chance, of accident. Pair was still a very young man; he must go on knocking, and some day — tomorrow, next week, next year, but some day certainly — the door of public favor would be opened to him. Meanwhile his position was by no means an unenviable one, goodness knows. To have your orbit in the art world of Paris, and to be recognized there as a star; to be written about in the " Revue des Deux-Mondes;" to possess the friendship of the masters, to know that they believe in you, to hear them prophesy, " He will do great things" — all that is something, even if your wares don't "take on" in the market-place.

"It's a good job, though, that I have n't got to live by them," Pair said; and there indeed he touched a salient point. His people were dead; his father had been a younger son; he had no money of his own. But his father's elder brother, a squire in Hampshire, made him rather a liberal allowance, — something like six hundred a year, I believe, which was opulence in the Latin Quarter. Now, the squire had been aware of Pair's relation with Godelinette from its inception, and had not disapproved. On his visits to Paris he had dined with them, given them dinners, and treated her with the utmost complaisance. But when, one fine morning, her tailor died, and my quixotic friend announced his intention of marrying her, dans les délais légaux the squire protested. I think I read the whole correspondence, and I remember that in the beginning the elder man took the tone of paradox and banter. "Behave dishonorably, my dear fellow. I have winked at your mistress heretofore, because boys will be boys; but it is the *man* who marries. And, anyhow, a woman is so much more interesting in a false position." But he soon became serious, presently furious, and, when the marriage was an accomplished fact, cut off the funds.

"Never mind, my dear," said Pair. "We will go to London and seek our fortune. We will write the songs of the people, and let who will make the laws. We will grow rich and famous, and

"When I am king, diddle-diddle,
You shall be queen!"

So they went to London to seek their fortune, and — that was the last I ever saw of them, nearly the last I heard. I had two letters from Pair, written within a month of their hegira, — gossipy, light-hearted letters, describing the people they were meeting, reporting Godelinette's quaint observations upon England and English things, explaining his hopes, his intentions, all very confidently, — and then I had no more. I wrote again, and still again, till, getting no answer, of course I ceased to write. I was hurt and puzzled; but in the spring we should meet in London, and could have it out. When the spring came, however, my plans were altered; I had to go to America.

I went by way of Havre, expecting to stay six weeks, and was gone six years.

On my return to England I said to people, "You have a brilliant young composer named Pair. Can you put me in the way of procuring his address?" The fortune he had come to seek he would surely have found; he would be a known man. But people looked blank, and declared they had never heard of him. I applied to music-publishers — with the same result. I wrote to his uncle in Hampshire; the squire did not reply. When I reached Paris I inquired of our friends there; they were as ignorant as I. "He must be dead," I concluded. "If he had lived, it is impossible we should not have heard of him." And I wondered what had become of Godelinette.

Then another eight or ten years passed, and now, in a waterside public at Bordeaux, an obscure old pianist was playing Pair's setting of "Lavender's blue," and stirring a hundred bitter-sweet, far-away memories of my friend. It was as if fifteen years were erased from my life. The face of Godelinette was palpable before me, — pale, with its sad little smile, its bright appealing eyes. Edmund might have been smoking across the table — I could hear his voice, I could have put out my hand and touched him. And all round me were the streets, the lights, the smells, the busy youthful va-et-vient of the Latin Quarter; and in my heart the yearning, half joy and all despair and anguish, with which we think of the old days when we were young, of how real and dear they were, of how irrecoverable they are.

And then the music stopped, the Brasserie des Quatre Vents became a glaring reality, and the painted female sipping eau-de-vie at my elbow remarked plaintively, 'Tu n'es pas rigolo, toi. Veux-tu faire une valse?'"

"I must speak to your musician," I said. "Excuse me."

He had played a bit of Pair's music. It was one chance in a thousand, but I wanted to ask him whether he could tell me anything about the composer. So I penetrated to the bottom of the shop, and approached his platform. He was bending over some sheets of music — making his next selection, doubtless.

"I beg your pardon —" I began.

He turned towards me. You will not be surprised — I was looking into Pair's own face.

You will not be surprised, but you will imagine what it was for me. Oh, yes, I recognized him instantly; there could be no mistake. And he recognized me, for he flushed, and winced, and started back.

I suppose for a little while we were both of us speechless, speechless and motionless, while our hearts stopped beating. By and by I think I said — something had to be said to break the situation — I think I said, "It's you, Edmund?" I remember he fumbled with a sheet of music, and kept his eyes bent on it, and muttered something inarticulate. Then there was another speechless, helpless suspension. He continued to fumble his music without looking up. At last I remember saying, through a sort of sickness and giddiness, "Let us get out of here — where we can talk."

"I can't leave yet. I've got another dance," he answered.

"Well, I'll wait," said I.

I sat down near him and waited, trying to create some kind of order out of the chaos in my mind, and half automatically watching and considering him as he played his dance, — Edmund Pair playing a dance for prostitutes and drunken sailors. He was not greatly changed. There were the same gray eyes, deep-set and wide apart, under the same broad forehead; the same fine nose and chin, the same sensitive mouth. The whole face was pretty much the same, only thinner perhaps, and with a look of apathy, of inanimation, that was foreign to my recollection of it. His hair had turned quite white, but otherwise he appeared no older than his years. His figure, tall, slender, well-knit, retained its vigor and its distinction. Though he wore a shabby brown Norfolk jacket, and his beard was two days old, you could in no circumstances have taken him for anything but a gentleman. I waited anxiously for the time when we should be alone, — anxiously, yet with a sort of terror. I was burning to understand, and yet I shrunk from doing so. If to conjecture even vaguely what experiences could have brought him to this, what dark things suffered or done, had been melancholy when he was a nameless old musician, now it was apalling, and I dreaded the explanation that I longed to hear.

At last he struck his final chord, and rose from the piano. Then he turned to me and said, composedly enough, "Well, I'm ready." He apparently had in some measure pulled himself together. In the street he took my arm. "Let's walk in this direction," he said, leading off, "towards the Christian quarter of the town." And in a moment he went on: "This has been an odd meeting. What brings you to Bordeaux?"

I explained that I was on my way to Biarritz, stopping for the night between two trains.

"Then it's all the more surprising that you should have stumbled into the Brasserie des Quatre Vents. You've altered very slightly. The world wags well with you? You look prosperous."

I cried out some incoherent protest. Afterwards I said: "You know what I want to hear. What does this mean?"

He laughed nervously. "Oh, the meaning's clear enough. It speaks for itself."

"I don't understand," said I.

"I'm pianist to the Brasserie des Quatre Vents. You saw me in the discharge of my duties."

"I don't understand," I repeated helplessly.

"And yet the inference is plain. What could have brought a man to such a pass save drink or evil courses?"

"Oh, don't trifle," I implored him.

"I'm not trifling. That's the worst of it. For I don't drink, and I'm not conscious of having pursued any especially evil courses."

"Well?" I questioned. "Well?"

"The fact of the matter simply is that I'm what they call a failure. I never came off."

"I don't understand," I repeated for a third time.

"No more do I, if you come to that. It's the will of Heaven, I suppose. Anyhow, it can't puzzle you more than it puzzles me. It seems contrary to the whole logic of circumstances, but it's the fact."

Thus far he had spoken listlessly, with a sort of bitter levity, an affectation of indifference; but after a little silence his mood appeared to change. His hand upon my arm tightened its grasp, and he began to speak rapidly, feelingly.

"Do you realize that it is nearly fifteen years since we have seen each other? The history of those fifteen years, so far as I am concerned, has been the history of a single uninterrupted déveine — one continuous run of ill-luck, against every probability of the game, against every effort I could make to play my cards effectively. When I started out, one might have thought, I had the best of chances. I had studied hard, I worked hard; I surely had as much general intelligence, as much special knowledge, as much apparent talent, as my competitors. And the stuff I produced seemed good to you, to my friends, and not wholly bad to me. It was musicianly, it was melodious, it was sincere; the critics all praised it; but — it never took on! The public would n't have it. What did it lack? I don't know. At last I could n't even get it published — invisible ink! And I had a wife to support."

He paused for a minute; then: "You see," he said, "we made the mistake, when we were young, of believing, against wise authority, that it *was* in mortals to command success, that he could command it who deserved it. We believed that the race would be to the swift, the battle to the strong; that a man was responsible for his own destiny, that he'd get what he merited. We believed that honest labor could n't go unrewarded. An immense mistake. Success is an affair of temperament, like faith, like love, like the color of your hair. Oh, the old story about industry, resolution, and no vices! I was industrious, I was resolute, and I had no more than the common share of vices. But I had the unsuccessful temperament;. and here I am. If my motives had been ignoble — but I can't see that they were. I wanted to earn a decent living; I wanted to justify my existence by doing something worthy of the world's acceptance. But the stars in their courses fought against me. I have tried hard to convince myself that the music I wrote was rubbish. It had its faults, no doubt. It was n't great, it was n't epoch-making. But, as music goes nowadays, it was jolly good. It was a jolly sight better than the average."

"Oh, that is certain, that is certain," I exclaimed, as he paused again.

"Well, anyhow, it did n't sell, and at last I could n't even get it published. So then I tried to find other work. I tried everything. I tried to teach — harmony and the theory of composition. I could n't get pupils. So few people want to study that sort of thing, and there were good masters already in the place. If I had known how to play, indeed! But I was never better than a fifth-rate executant; I had never gone in for that; my "lay" was composition. I could n't give piano lessons, I could n't play in public — unless in a gargotte like the hole we have just left. Oh, I tried everything. I tried to get musical criticism to do for the newspapers. Surely I was competent to do musical criticism. But no — they would n't employ me. I had ill luck, ill luck, ill luck — nothing but ill luck, defeat, disappointment. Was it the will of Heaven? I wondered what unforgivable sin I had committed to be punished so. Do you know what it is like to work and pray and wait, day after day, and watch day after day come and go and bring you nothing? Oh, I tasted the whole heart-sickness of hope deferred; Giant Despair was my constant bedfellow."

"But — with your connections —" I began.

"Oh, my connections!" he cried. "There was the rub. London is the cruellest town in Europe. For sheer cold blood and heartlessness give Londoners the palm. I had connections enough for the first month or so, and then people found out things that did n't concern them. They found out some things that were true, and they imagined other things that were false. They would n't have my wife; they told the most infamous lies about her; and I would n't have *them*. Could I be civil to people who insulted and slandered *her?* I had no connections in London, except with the under-world. I got down to copying parts for theatrical orchestras, and, working twelve hours a day, earned about thirty shillings a week."

"You might have come back to Paris."

"And fared worse. I could n't have earned thirty pence in Paris. Mind you, the only trade I had learned was that of a musical composer; and I could n't compose music that people would buy. I should have starved as a copyist in Paris, where copyists are more numerous and worse paid. Teach there? But to one competent master of harmony in London there are ten in Paris. No; it was a hopeless case."

"It is incomprehensible — incomprehensible," said I.

"But wait — wait till you've heard the end. One

would think I had had enough — not so! One would think my cup of bitterness was full. No fear! There was a stronger cup still a-brewing for me. When Fortune takes a grudge against a man, she never lets up. She exacts the uttermost farthing. I was pretty badly off, but I had one treasure left — I had Godelinette. I used to think that she was my compensation. I would say to myself, 'A man can't have all blessings. How can you expect others, when you've got her?' And I would accuse myself of ingratitude for complaining of my unsuccess. Then she fell ill. My God, how I watched over, prayed over her! It seemed impossible — I could not believe — that she would be taken from me. Yet, Harry, do you know what that poor child was thinking? Do you know what her dying thoughts were — her wishes? Throughout her long painful illness she was thinking that she was an obstacle in my way, a weight upon me; that if it were n't for her, I should get on, have friends, a position; that it would be a good thing for me if she should die; and she was hoping in her poor little heart that she would n't get well! Oh, I know it, I knew it — and you see me here alive. She let herself die for my sake — as if I could care for anything without her. That's what brought us here, to France, to Bordeaux — her illness. The doctors said she must pass the spring out of England, away from the March winds, in the South; and I begged and borrowed money enough to take her. And we were on our way to Arcachon; but when we reached Bordeaux she was too ill to continue the journey, and — she died here."

We walked on for some distance in silence, then he

added: "That was four years ago. You wonder why I live to tell you of it, why I have n't cut my throat. I don't know whether it's cowardice or conscientious scruples. It seems rather inconsequent to say that I believe in a God, does n't it? — that I believe one's life is not one's own to make an end of? Anyhow, here I am, keeping body and soul together as musician to a brasserie-à-femmes. I can't go back to England, I can't leave Bordeaux — she's buried here. I've hunted high and low for work, and found it nowhere save in the brasserie-à-femmes. With that, and a little copying now and then, I manage to pay my way."

"But your uncle?" I asked.

"Do you think I would touch a penny of his money?" Pair retorted, almost fiercely. "It was he who began it. My wife let herself die. It was virtual suicide. It was he who created the situation that drove her to it."

"You are his heir, though, are n't you?"

"No, the estates are not entailed."

We had arrived at the door of my hotel. "Well, good-night and bon voyage," he said.

"You need n't wish me bon voyage," I answered. "Of course I'm not leaving Bordeaux for the present."

"Oh, yes, you are. You're going on to Biarritz to-morrow morning, as you intended."

And herewith began a long and most painful struggle. I could persuade him to accept no help of any sort from me. "What I can't do for myself," he declared, "I'll do without. My dear fellow, all that you propose is contrary to the laws of Nature. One man can't keep another — it's an impossible relation.

And I won't be kept; I won't be a burden. Besides, to tell you the truth, I've got past caring. The situation you find me in seems terrible to you; to me it's no worse than another. You see, I'm hardened; I've got past caring."

"At any rate," I insisted, "I shan't go on to Biarritz. "I'll spend my holiday here, and we can see each other every day. What time shall we meet to-morrow?"

"No, no, I can't meet you again. Don't ask me to; you mean it kindly, I know, but you're mistaken. It's done me good to talk it all out to you, but I can't meet you again. I've got no heart for friendship, and — you remind me too keenly of many things."

"But if I come to the brasserie to-morrow night?"

"Oh, if you do that, you'll oblige me to throw up my employment there, and hide from you. You must promise not to come again — you must respect my wishes."

"You're cruel, you know."

"Perhaps, perhaps. But I think I'm only reasonable. Anyhow, good-bye."

He shook my hand hurriedly, and moved off. What could I do? I stood looking after him till he had vanished in the night, with a miserable baffled recognition of my helplessness to help him.

A RESPONSIBILITY.

A RESPONSIBILITY.

It has been an episode like a German sentence, with its predicate at the end. Trifling incidents occurred at haphazard, as it seemed, and I never guessed they were by way of making sense. Then, this morning, somewhat of the suddenest, came the verb and the full stop.

Yesterday I should have said there was nothing to tell; to-day there is too much. The announcement of his death has caused me to review our relations, with the result of discovering my own part to have been that of an accessory before the fact. I did not kill him (though, even there, I'm not sure I didn't lend a hand), but I might have saved his life. It is certain that he made me signals of distress — faint, shy, tentative, but unmistakable — and that I pretended not to understand: just barely dipped my colors, and kept my course. Oh, if I had dreamed that his distress was extreme — that he was on the point of foundering and going down! However, that does n't exonerate me; I ought to have turned aside to find out. It was a case of criminal negligence. That he, poor man, probably never blamed me, only adds to the burden on my conscience. He had got past blaming people, I dare say, and doubtless merely lumped me with the rest — with the sum-total of things that made life unsupportable. Yet, for a moment, when we first met, his face showed a distinct glimmering of hope; so perhaps there was a distinct disappointment. He must have had so many disappointments before it came to — what it came to; but it would n't have come to that if he had got hardened to them. Possibly they had lost their outlines, and merged into one dull general disappointment that was too hard to bear. I wonder whether the Priest and the Levite were smitten with remorse after they had passed on. Unfortunately, in this instance, no good Samaritan followed.

The bottom of our long table d'hôte was held by a Frenchman, a Normand, a giant, but a pallid and rather flabby giant, whose name, if he had another than Monsieur, I never heard. He professed to be a painter, used to sketch birds and profiles on the back of his menu-card between the courses, wore shamelessly the multi-colored rosette of a foreign order in his buttonhole, and talked with a good deal of physiognomy. I had the corner seat at his right, and was flanked in turn by Miss Etta J. Hicks, a bouncing young person from Chicago, beyond whom, like rabbits in a company of foxes, cowered Mr. and Mrs. Jordan P. Hicks, two broken-spirited American parents. At Monsieur's left, and facing me, sat Colonel Escott, very red and cheerful; then a young man who called the Colonel Cornel, and came from Dublin, proclaiming himself a barr'ster, and giving his name as Flarty, though on his card it was written Flaherty; and then Sir Richard Maistre. After him, a diminishing perspective of busy diners — for purposes of conversation, so far as we were concerned, inhabitants of the Fourth Dimension.

Of our immediate constellation, Sir Richard Maistre

was the only member on whom the eye was tempted to linger. The others were obvious — simple equations, soluble "in the head." But he called for slate and pencil, offered materials for doubt and speculation, though it would not have been easy to tell wherein they lay. What displayed itself to a cursory inspection was quite unremarkable — simply a decent-looking young Englishman, of medium stature, with square-cut plain features, reddish-brown hair, gray eyes, and clothes and manners of the usual pattern. Yet, showing through this ordinary surface, there was something cryptic. For me, at any rate, it required a constant effort not to stare at him. I felt it from the beginning, and I felt it to the end — a teasing curiosity, a sort of magnetism that drew my eyes in his direction. I was always on my guard to resist it, and that was really the inception of my neglect of him. From I don't know what stupid motive of pride, I was anxious that he should n't discern the interest he had excited in me; so I paid less ostensible attention to him than to the others, who excited none at all. I tried to appear unconscious of him as a detached personality, to treat him as merely a part of the group as a whole. Then I improved such occasions as presented themselves to steal glances at him, study him à la dérobée — groping after the quality, whatever it was, that made him a puzzle — seeking to formulate, to classify him.

Already, at the end of my first dinner, he had singled himself out and left an impression. I went into the smoking-room, and began to wonder, over a cup of coffee and a cigarette, who he was. I had not heard his voice; he had n't talked much, and his few observations had been murmured into the ears of his next neighbors. All the same, he had left an impression, and I found myself wondering who he was, the young man with the square-cut features and the reddish-brown hair. I have said that his features were square-cut and plain, but they were small and carefully finished, and as far as possible from being common. And his gray eyes, though not conspicuous for size or beauty, had a character, an expression. They *said* something — something I couldn't perfectly translate, something shrewd, humorous, even perhaps a little caustic, and yet sad; not violently, not rebelliously sad (I should never have dreamed that it was a sadness which would drive him to desperate remedies), but rather resignedly, submissively sad, as if he had made up his mind to put the best face on a sorry business. This was carried out by a certain abruptness, a slight lack of suavity, in his movements, in his manner of turning his head, of using his hands. It hinted a degree of determination which, in the circumstances, seemed superfluous. He had unfolded his napkin and attacked his dinner with an air of resolution, like a man with a task before him, who mutters, "Well, it's got to be done, and I'll do it." At a hazard, he was two- or three-and-thirty, but below his neck he looked older. He was dressed like everybody, but his costume had, somehow, an effect of soberness beyond his years. It was decidedly not smart, and smartness was the dominant note at the Hôtel d'Angleterre.

I was still more or less vaguely ruminating him, in a corner of the smoking-room, on that first evening, when I became aware that he was standing near me. As I looked up, our eyes met, and for the fraction of a second fixed each other. It was barely the fraction of a second, but it was time enough for the transmission of a message. I knew as certainly as if he had said so that he wanted to speak, to break the ice, to scrape an acquaintance; I knew that he had approached me, and was loitering in my neighborhood for that specific purpose. I *don't* know, I have studied the psychology of the moment in vain to understand, why I felt a perverse impulse to put him off. I was interested in him, I was curious about him; and there he stood, testifying that the interest was reciprocal, ready to make the advances, only waiting for a glance or a motion of encouragement; and I deliberately secluded myself behind my coffee-cup and my cigarette smoke. I suppose it was the working of some obscure mannish vanity — of what in a woman would have defined itself as coyness and coquetry. If he wanted to speak — well, let him speak; I wouldn't help him. I could realize the processes of *his* mind even more clearly than those of my own — his desire, his hesitancy. He was too timid to leap the barriers; I must open a gate for him. He hovered near me for a minute longer, and then drifted away. I felt his disappointment, his spiritual shrug of the shoulders; and I perceived rather suddenly that I was disappointed myself. I must have been hoping all along that he would speak quand même, and now I was moved to run after him, to call him back. That, however, would imply a consciousness of guilt, an admission that my attitude had been intentional; so I kept my seat, making a mental rendezvous with him for the morrow.

Between my Irish vis-à-vis, Flaherty, and myself there existed no such strain. He presently sauntered up to me, and dropped into conversation as easily as if we had been old friends.

"Well, and are you here for your health or your entertainment?" he began. "But I don't need to ask that of a man who's drinking black coffee and smoking tobacco at this hour of the night. I'm the only invalid at our end of the table, and I'm no better than an amateur meself. It's a barrister's throat I have — I caught it waiting for briefs in me chambers at Doblin."

We chatted together for a half-hour or so, and before we parted he had given me a good deal of general information — about the town, the natives, the visitors, the sands, the golf-links, the hunting, and, with the rest, about our neighbors at table.

"Did ye notice the pink-faced bald little man at me right? That's Cornel Escott, C.B., retired. He takes a sea-bath every morning, to live up to the letters; and, faith, it's an act of heroism, no less, in weather the like of this. Three weeks have I been here, and but wan day of sunshine, and the mercury never above fifty. The other fellow, him at me left, is what you'd be slow to suspect by the look of him, I'll go bail; and that's a bar'net, Sir Richard Maistre, with a place in Hampshire, and ten thousand a year if he's a penny. The young lady beside yourself rejoices in the euphonious name of Hicks, and trains her Popper and Mommer behind her like slaves in a Roman triumph. They're Americans, if you must have the truth, though I oughtn't to tell it on them, for I'm an Irishman myself, and it's not for the pot to be bearing tales of the kettle. However, their tongues bewray them; so I've violated no confidence."

The knowledge that my young man was a baronet with a place in Hampshire somewhat disenchanted me. A baronet with a place in Hampshire left too little to the imagination. The description seemed to curtail his potentialities, to prescribe his orbit, to connote turnip-fields, house-parties, and a whole system of British commonplace. Yet, when, the next day at luncheon, I again had him before me in the flesh, my interest revived. Its lapse had been due to an association of ideas which I now recognized as unscientific. A baronet with twenty places in Hampshire would remain at the end of them all a human being; and no human being could be finished off in a formula of half a dozen words. Sir Richard Maistre, anyhow, couldn't be. He was enigmatic, and his effect upon me was enigmatic too. Why did I feel that tantalizing inclination to stare at him, coupled with that reluctance frankly to engage in talk with him? Why did he attack his luncheon with that appearance of grim resolution? For a minute, after he had taken his seat, he eyed his knife, fork, and napkin, as a laborer might a load that he had to lift, measuring the difficulties he must cope with; then he gave his head a resolute nod, and set to work. To-day, as yesterday, he said very little, murmured an occasional remark into the ear of Flaherty, accompanying it usually with a sudden short smile; but he listened to everything, and did so with apparent appreciation.

Our proceedings were opened by Miss Hicks, who

asked Colonel Escott, "Well, Colonel, have you had your bath this morning?"

The Colonel chuckled, and answered, "Oh, yes — yes, yes — couldn't forego my bath, you know — couldn't possibly forego my bath."

"And what was the temperature of the water?" she continued.

"Fifty-two — fifty-two — three degrees warmer than the air — three degrees," responded the Colonel, still chuckling, as if the whole affair had been extremely funny.

"And you, Mr. Flaherty, I suppose you've been to Bayonne?"

"No, I've broken me habit, and not left the hotel."

Subsequent experience taught me that these were conventional modes by which the conversation was launched every day, like the preliminary moves in chess. We had another ritual for dinner; Miss Hicks then inquired if the Colonel had taken his ride, and Flaherty played his game of golf. The next inevitable step was common to both meals. Colonel Escott would pour himself a glass of the vin ordinaire, a jug of which was set by every plate, and, holding it up to the light, exclaim with simulated gusto, "Ah! Fine old wine! Remarkably full rich flavor!" At this pleasantry we would all gently laugh; and the word was free.

Sir Richard, as I have said, appeared to be an attentive and appreciative listener, not above smiling at our mildest sallies; but, watching him out of the corner of an eye, I noticed that my own observations seemed to strike him with peculiar force — which led me to talk *at* him. Why not to him, with him? The interest was reciprocal; he would have liked a dialogue; he would have welcomed a chance to commence one; and I could at any instant have given him such a chance. I talked *at* him, it is true; but I talked *with* Flaherty or Miss Hicks, or *to* the company at large. Of his separate identity he had no reason to believe me conscious. From a mixture of motives, in which I'm not sure that a certain heathenish enjoyment of his embarrassment didn't count for something, I was determined that if he wanted to know me he must come the whole distance; I wouldn't meet him half-way. Of course I had no idea that it could be a matter of the faintest real importance to the man. I judged his feelings by my own; and though I was interested in him, I shall have conveyed an altogether exaggerated notion of my interest if you fancy it kept me awake at night. How was I to guess that *his* case was more serious, — that he was not simply desirous of a little amusing talk, but starving, starving for a little human sympathy, a little brotherly love and comradeship? — that he was in an abnormally sensitive condition of mind, where mere negative unresponsiveness could hurt him like a slight or a rebuff?

In the course of the week I ran over to Pau, to pass a day with the Winchfields, who had a villa there. When I came back I brought with me all that they (who knew everybody) could tell about Sir Richard Maistre. He was intelligent and amiable, but the shyest of shy men. He avoided general society, frightened away perhaps by the British Mamma, and spent a good part of each year abroad, wandering rather listlessly from town to town. Though young and rich, he was neither fast nor ambitious: the Members' entrance to the House of Commons, the stage-doors of the music halls, were equally without glamour for him; and if he was a Justice of the Peace and a Deputy Lieutenant, he had become so through the tacit operation of his stake in the country. He had chambers in St. James's Street, was a member of the Travellers Club, and played the violin — for an amateur rather well. His brother, Mortimer Maistre, was in diplomacy — at Rio Janeiro or somewhere. His sister had married an Australian, and lived in Melbourne.

At the Hôtel d'Angleterre I found his shyness was mistaken for indifference. He was civil to everybody, but intimate with none. He attached himself to no party, paired off with no individuals. He sought nobody. On the other hand, the persons who went out of their way to seek him, came back, as they felt, repulsed. He had been polite, but languid. These, however, were not the sort of persons he would be likely to care for. There prevailed a general conception of him as cold, unsociable. He certainly walked about a good deal alone — you met him on the sands, on the cliffs, in the stiff little streets, rambling aimlessly, seldom with a companion. But to me it was patent that he played the solitary from necessity, not from choice — from the necessity of his temperament. A companion was precisely that which above all things his heart coveted; only he didn't know how to set about annexing one. If he sought nobody, it was because he didn't know how. This was a part of what his eyes said; they bespoke his desire, his perplexity, his lack of nerve. Of the people who put themselves out to seek him, there was Miss Hicks; there were a family from Leeds, named Bunn, a father, mother, son, and two redoubtable daughters, who drank champagne with every meal, dressed in the height of fashion, said their say at the tops of their voices, and were understood to be auctioneers; a family from Bayswater named Krausskopf. I was among those whom he had marked as men he would like to fraternize with. As often as our paths crossed, his eyes told me that he longed to stop and speak, and continue the promenade abreast. I was under the control of a demon of mischief; I took a malicious pleasure in eluding and baffling him — in passing on with a nod. It had become a kind of game; I was curious to see whether he would ever develop sufficient hardihood to take the bull by the horns. After all, from a conventional point of view, my conduct was quite justifiable. I always meant to do better by him next time, and then I always deferred it to the next. But, from a conventional point of view, my conduct was quite unassailable. I said this to myself when I had momentary qualms of conscience. Now, rather late in the day, it strikes me that the conventional point of view should have been readjusted to the special case. I should have allowed for his personal equation.

My cousin Wilford came to Biarritz about this time, stopping for a week, on his way home from a tour in Spain. I could n't find a room for him at the Hôtel d'Angleterre, so he put up at a rival hostelry over the way; but he dined with me on the evening of his arrival, a place being made for him between mine and Monsieur's. He had n't been at the table five

minutes before the rumor went abroad who he was —
somebody had recognized him. Then those who
were within reach of his voice listened with all
their ears — Colonel Escott, Flaherty, Maistre, and
Miss Hicks, of course, who even called him by name:
"Oh, Mr. Wilford," "Now, Mr. Wilford," &c. After
dinner, in the smoking-room, a cluster of people hung
round us; men with whom I had no acquaintance
came merrily up and asked to be introduced. Colonel
Escott and Flaherty joined us. At the outskirts of
the group I beheld Sir Richard Maistre. His eyes
(without his realizing it perhaps) begged me to invite
him, to present him; and I affected not to understand! This is one of the little things I find hardest
to forgive myself. My whole behavior towards the
young man is now a subject of self-reproach; if it had
been different, who knows that the tragedy of yesterday would ever have happened? If I had answered
his timid overtures, walked with him, talked with
him, cultivated his friendship, given him mine, established a kindly human relation with him, I can't help
feeling that he might not have got to such a desperate pass, that I might have cheered him, helped him,
saved him. I feel it especially when I think of Wilford. His eyes attested so much; he would have enjoyed meeting him so keenly. No doubt he was
already fond of the man, had loved him through his
books, like so many others. If I had introduced him?
If we had taken him with us the next morning on our
excursion to Cambo? Included him occasionally in
our smokes and parleys?

Wilford left for England without dining again at
the Hôtel d'Angleterre. We were busy "doing" the

country, and never chanced to be at Biarritz at the dinner hour. During that week I scarcely saw Sir Richard Maistre.

Another little circumstance that rankles especially now would have been ridiculous except for the way things have ended. It is n't easy to tell — it was so petty and I am so ashamed. Colonel Escott had been abusing London, describing it as the least beautiful of the capitals of Europe, comparing it unfavorably to Paris, Vienna, and St. Petersburg. I took up the cudgels in its defence, mentioned its atmosphere, its tone; Paris, Vienna, St. Petersburg were lyric, London was epic; and so forth and so forth. Then, shifting from the æsthetic to the utilitarian, I argued that of all great towns it was the healthiest, its death-rate was lowest. Sir Richard Maistre had followed my dissertation attentively, and with a countenance that signified approval; and when, with my reference to the death-rate, I paused, he suddenly burned his ships. He looked me full in the eye, and said, "Thirty-seven, I believe?" His heightened color, a nervous movement of the lip, betrayed the effort it had cost him; but at last he had *done it* — screwed his courage to the sticking-place, and spoken. And I — I can never forget it — I grow hot when I think of it — but I was possessed by a devil. His eyes hung on my face, awaiting my response, pleading for a cue. "Go on," they urged. "I have taken the first, the difficult step — make the next smoother for me." And I — I answered lackadaisically with just a casual glance at him, "I don't know the figures," and absorbed myself in my viands.

Two or three days later his place was filled by a

stranger, and Flaherty told me that he had left for the Riviera.

All this happened last March at Biarritz. I never saw him again till three weeks ago. It was one of those frightfully hot afternoons in July; I had come out of my club, and was walking up St. James's Street, towards Piccadilly; he was moving in an opposite sense; and thus we approached each other. He did n't see me, however, till we had drawn rather near to a conjunction: then he gave a little start of recognition, his eyes brightened, his pace slackened, his right hand prepared to advance itself — and I bowed slightly, and pursued my way! Don't ask why I did it. It is enough to confess it without having to explain it. I glanced backwards, by and by, over my shoulder. He was standing where I had met him, half turned round, and looking after me. But when he saw that I was observing him, he hastily shifted about, and continued his descent of the street.

That was only three weeks ago. Only three weeks ago I still had it in my power to act. I am sure — I don't know why I am sure, but I *am* sure — that I could have deterred him. For all that one can gather from the brief note he left behind, it seems he had no special, definite motive; he had met with no losses, got into no scrape; he was simply tired and sick of life and of himself. "I have no friends," he wrote. "Nobody will care. People don't like me; people avoid me. I have wondered why; I have tried to watch myself and discover; I have tried to be decent. I suppose it must be that I emit a repellent fluid; I suppose I am a 'bad sort.'" He had a morbid notion that people did n't like him, that people avoided him!

Oh, to be sure, there were the Bunns and the Krausskopfs and their ilk, plentiful enough: but he understood what it was that attracted *them*. Other people, the people *he* could have liked, kept their distance — were civil, indeed, but reserved. He wanted bread, and they gave him a stone. It never struck him, I suppose, that they attributed the reserve to him. But I — I knew that his reserve was only an effect of his shyness; I *knew* that he wanted bread: and that knowledge constituted my moral responsibility. I did n't know that his need was extreme; but I have tried in vain to absolve myself with the reflection. I ought to have made inquiries. When I think of that afternoon in St. James's Street — only three weeks ago — I feel like an assassin. The vision of him, as he stopped and looked after me — I can't banish it. Why did n't some good spirit move me to turn back and overtake him?

It is so hard for the mind to reconcile itself to the irretrievable. I can't shake off a sense that there is something to be done. I can't realize that it is too late.

CASTLES NEAR SPAIN.

CASTLES NEAR SPAIN.

I

THAT he should not have guessed it from the beginning seems odd, if you like, until one stops to consider the matter twice; then, I think, one sees that after all there was no shadow of a reason why he should have done so, — one sees, indeed, that even had a suspicion of the truth at any time crossed his mind, he would have had the best of reasons for scouting it as nonsense. It is obvious to us from the first word, because we know instinctively that otherwise there would be no story; it is that which knits a mere sequence of incidents into a coherent, communicable whole. But, to his perceptions, the thing never presented itself as a story at all. It was n't an anecdote which somebody had buttonholed him to tell; it was an adventure in which he found himself launched, an experience to be enjoyed bit by bit, as it befell, but in no wise suggestive of any single specific climax. What earthly hint had he received from which to infer the identity of the two women? On the contrary, were n't the actions of the one totally inconsistent with what everybody assured him was the manner of life — with what the necessities of the case led him to believe would be the condition of spirit — of the other? If the tale were to be published, the fun would lie, not in attempting to mystify the reader, but in watching with him the mystification of the hero, — in showing how he played at hoodman-blind with his destiny, and how surprised he was, when, the bandage stripped from his eyes, he saw whom he had caught.

II

On that first morning, — the first after his arrival at Saint-Graal, and the first, also, of the many on which they encountered each other in the forest, — he was bent upon a sentimental pilgrimage to Granjolaye. He was partly obeying, partly seeking, an emotion. His mind, inevitably, was full of old memories; the melancholy by which they were attended he found distinctly pleasant, and was inclined to nurse. To revisit the scene of their boy-and-girl romance, would itself be romantic. In a little while he would come to the park gates, and could look up the long straight avenue to the château, — there where, when they were children, twenty years ago, he and she had played so earnestly at being married, burning for each other with one of those strange, inarticulate passions that almost every childhood knows; and where now, worse than widowed, she withheld herself, in silent, mysterious, tragical seclusion.

And then he heard the rhythm of a horse's hoofs; and looking forward, down the green pathway, between the two walls of forest, he saw a lady cantering towards him.

In an instant she had passed; and it took a little while for the blur of black and white that she had flashed upon his retina to clear into an image, — which even then, from under-exposure, was obscure and piecemeal: a black riding-habit, of some flexile stuff that fluttered in a multitude of pretty curves and folds; a small black hat, a toque, set upon a loosely fastened mass of black hair; a face intensely white — a softly rounded face, but intensely white; soft full lips, singularly scarlet; and large eyes, very dark.

It was not much, certainly, but it persisted. The impression, defective as I give it, had been pleasing; an impression of warm femininity, of graceful motion. It had had the quality, besides, of the unexpected and the fugitive, and the advantage of a sylvan background. Anyhow, it pursued him. He went on to his journey's end; stopped before the great gilded grille, with its multiplicity of scrolls and flourishes, its coronets and interlaced initials; gazed up the shadowy aisle of plane-trees to the bit of castle gleaming in the sun at the end; remembered the child Hélène, and how he and she had loved each other there, a hundred years ago; and thought of the exiled, worse than widowed woman immured there now: but it was mere remembering, mere thinking, it was mere cerebration. The emotion he had looked for did not come. An essential part of him was elsewhere, — following the pale lady in the black riding-habit, trying to get a clearer vision of her face, blaming him for his inattention when she had been palpable before him, wondering who she was.

"If she should prove to be a neighbor, I sha'n't bore myself so dreadfully down here after all," he thought. "I wonder if I shall meet her again as I go home." She would very likely be returning the way she had gone. But, though he loitered, he did not meet her again. He met nobody. It was, in some measure, the attraction of that lonely forest lane that one almost never did meet anybody in it.

III

At Saint-Graal André was waiting to lunch with him.

"When we were children," Paul wrote in a letter to Mrs. Winchfield, "André, our gardener's son, and I were as intimate as brothers, he being the only companion of my sex and age the neighborhood afforded. But now, after a separation of twenty years, André, who has become our curé, insists upon treating me with distance. He won't waive the fact that I am the lord of the manor, and calls me relentlessly Monsieur. I've done everything to entice him to unbend, but his backbone is of granite. From the merriest of mischief-loving youngsters, he has hardened into the solemnest of square-toes, with *such* a long upper-lip, and manners as stiff as the stuff of his awful best cassock, which he always buckles on prior to paying me a visit. Whatever is a poor young man to do? At our first meeting, after my arrival, I fell upon his neck, and thee-and-thou'd him, as of old time; he repulsed me with a vous italicized. At last I demanded reason. 'Why *will* you treat me with this inexorable respect? What have I done to deserve it? What can I do to forfeit it?' Il devint cramoisi (in the traditional phrase) and stared. — This is what it is to come back to the home of your infancy."

André, in his awful best cassock, was waiting on the terrace. It was on the terrace that Paul had ordered luncheon to be served. The terrace at Saint-Graal is a very jolly place. It stretches the whole length of the southern façade of the house, and is generously broad. It is paved with great lozenge-shaped slabs of marble, stained in delicate pinks and grays with lichens; and a marble balustrade borders it, overgrown, the columns half uprooted and twisted from the perpendicular, by an aged wistaria-vine, with a trunk as stout as a tree's. Seated there, one can look off over miles of richly-timbered country, dotted with white-walled villages, and traversed by the Nive and the Adour, to the wry masses of the Pyrenees, purple curtains hiding Spain.

Here, under an awning, the table was set, gay with white linen and glistening glass and silver, a centrepiece of flowers and jugs of red and yellow wine. The wistaria was in blossom, a world of color and fragrance, shaken at odd moments by the swift dartings of innumerable lizards. The sun shone hot and clear; the still air, as you touched it, felt like velvet.

"Oh, what a heavenly place, what a heavenly day!" cried Paul; "it only needs a woman." And then, meeting André's eye, he caught himself up, with a gesture of contrition. "I beg a thousand pardons. I forgot your cloth. If you," he added, "would only forget it too, what larks we might have together. Allons, à table."

And they sat down.

If Paul had sincerely wished to forfeit André's respect, he could scarcely have employed more efficacious means to do so, than his speech and conduct throughout the meal that followed. You know how flippant, how "fly-away," he can be when the mood seizes him, how whole-heartedly he can play the fool. To-day he really behaved outrageously; and, since the priest maintained a straight countenance, I think the wonder is that he did n't excommunicate him.

"I remember you were a teetotaller, André, when you were young," his host began, pushing a decanter towards him.

"That, monsieur, was because my mother wished it, and my father was a drunkard," André answered bluntly. "Since my father's death, I have taken wine in moderation." He filled his glass.

"I remember once I cooked some chestnuts over a spirit-stove, and you refused to touch them, on the ground that they were alcoholic."

"That would have been from a confusion of thought," the curé explained, with never a smile. "But it was better to err on the side of scrupulosity than on that of self-indulgence."

"Ah, that depends. That depends on whether the pleasure you got from your renunciation equalled that you might have got from the chestnuts."

"You 're preaching pure Paganism."

"Oh, I 'm not denying I 'm a Pagan — in my amateurish way. Let me give you some asparagus. Do you think a man can be saved who smokes cigarettes between the courses?"

"Saved?" questioned André. "What have cigarettes to do with a man's salvation?"

"It 's a habit I learned in Russia. I feared it might relate itself in some way to the Schism." And he lit a cigarette. "I 'm always a rigid Catholic when I 'm in France."

"And when you're in England?"

"Oh, one goes in for local color, for picturesqueness, don't you know. The Church of England's charmingly overgrown with ivy. And besides, they're going to disestablish it. One must make the most of it while it lasts. Tell me — why can you never get decent brioches except in Catholic countries?"

"Is that a fact?"

"I swear it."

"It's very singular," said André.

"It's only one of the many odd things a fellow learns from travel. — Hush! Wait a moment."

He rose hastily, and made a dash with his hand at the tail of a lizard that was hanging temptingly out from a bunch of wistaria leaves. But the lizard was too quick for him. With a whisk, it had disappeared. He sank back into his chair, sighing. "It's always like that. They'll never keep still long enough to let me catch them. What's the use of a university education and a cosmopolitan culture, if you can't catch lizards? Do you think they have eyes in the backs of their heads?"

André stared.

"Oh, I see. You think I'm frivolous," Paul said plaintively. "But you ought to have seen me an hour or two ago."

André's eyes asked, "Why?"

"Oh, I was plunged in all the most appropriate emotions — shedding floods of tears over my lost childhood and my misspent youth. Don't you like to have a good cry now and then? Oh, I don't mean literal tears, of course; only spiritual ones. For the letter killeth, but the spirit giveth life. I walked over to Granjolaye."

André looked surprise. "To Granjolaye? Have you — were you —"

He hesitated, but Paul understood. "Have you heard from her? Were you invited?" "Oh, dear, no," he answered. "No such luck. Not to the Château, only to the gates — the East Gate." (The principal entrance to the home part of Granjolaye is the South Gate, which opens upon the Route Départementale.) "I stood respectfully outside, and looked through the grating of the grille. I walked through the forest, by the Sentier des Contrebandiers."

"Ah," said André.

"And on my way what do you suppose I met?"

"A — a viper," responded André. "The hot weather is bringing them out. I killed two in my garden yesterday."

"Oh, you cruel thing! What did you want to kill the poor young creatures for? And then to boast of it! — But no, not a viper. A lady."

"A lady?"

"Yes — a real lady; she wore gloves. She was riding. I hope you won't think I'm asking impertinent questions, but I wonder if you can tell me who she is."

"A lady riding in the Sentier des Contrebandiers?" André repeated incredulously.

"She looked like one. Of course I may have been deceived. I didn't hear her speak. Do you think she was a cook?"

"I didn't know any one ever rode in the Sentier des Contrebandiers."

"Oh, for that, I give you my word of honor. A lady — or say a female — in a black riding-habit; dark hair and eyes; very pale, with red lips and things. Oh, I'm not trying to impose upon you. It was about half a mile this side of where the path skirts the road."

"You might stop in the Sentier des Contrebandiers from January to December and not meet a soul," said André.

"Ah, I see. There's no convincing you. Sceptic! And yet, twenty years ago, you'd have been pretty sure to meet a certain couple of small boys there, wouldn't you?"

"Si fait," assented André. "We went there a good deal. But we were privileged. The only boys in this country now are peasants' children, and they have no leisure for wandering in the wood. When they're not at school, they're working in the fields. As for their elders, the path is rough and circuitous; the high road's smoother and shorter, no matter where you're bound. Since our time, I doubt if twenty people have passed that way."

"That argues ill for people's taste. The place is lovely. Under foot, it's quite overgrown with mosses; and the branches interlace overhead. Where the sun filters through, you get adorable effects of light and shadow. It's fearfully romantic; perfect for making love in, and that sort of thing. Oh, if all the women hereabouts hadn't such hawk-like noses! You see, the Duke of Wellington was here in 1814. — No? He wasn't? I thought I'd read he was. — Ah, well, he was just over the border. But my lady of this morning hadn't a hawk-like nose. I can't quite remember what style of nose she did have, but it wasn't hawk-like. I say, frankly, as between old friends, have you any notion who she was?"

"What kind of horse had she?"

"Ah, there!" cried Paul, with a despairing gesture. "You've touched my vulnerable point. I never shall have any memory for horses. I think it was black — no, brown — no, gray — no, green. Oh, what am I saying? I can't remember. Do — do you make it an essential?"

"She might have been from Bayonne."

"Who rides from Bayonne? Fancy a Bayonnaise on a horse! They're all busy in their shops."

"You forget the military. She may have been the wife of an officer."

"Oh, horror! Do you really think so? Then she must have been frowsy and provincial, after all; and I thought her so smart and distinguished-looking and everything."

"Or perhaps an Englishwoman from Biarritz. They sometimes ride out as far as this."

"Dear André, if she were English, I should have known it at a glance — and there the matter would have rested. I have at least a practised eye for Englishwomen. I haven't lived half my life in England without learning something."

"Well, there are none but English at Biarritz at this season."

"She was never English. Don't try to bully *me*. Besides, she evidently knew the country. Otherwise, how could she have found the Sentier des Contrebandiers? — She wasn't from Granjolaye?"

"There's no one at Granjolaye save the Queen herself."

"Deceiver! Manuela told me last night. She has her little Court, her maids-of-honor. I think my inconnue looked like a maid-of-honor."

"She has her aunt, old Mademoiselle Henriette, and a couple of German women, countesses or baronesses or something, with unpronounceable names."

"I can't believe she's German. Still, I suppose there are some Christian Germans. Perhaps. . . ."

"They're both middle-aged. Past fifty, I should think."

"Oh. — Ah, well, that disposes of them. But how do you know her Majesty hasn't a friend, a guest, staying with her?"

"It's possible, but most unlikely, seeing the close retirement in which she lives. She's never once gone beyond her garden since she came back there, three, four years ago; nor received any visitors. Personne — not the Bishop of Bayonne nor the Sous-Préfet, not even feu Monsieur le Comte, though they all called, as a matter of civility. She has her private chaplain. If a guest had arrived at Granjolaye, the whole country would know it and talk of it."

"Oh, I see what you're trying to insinuate," cried Paul. "You're trying to insinuate that she came from Château Yroulte." That was the next nearest country-house.

"Nothing of the sort," said André. "Château Yroulte has been shut up and uninhabited these two years — ever since the death of old Monsieur Raoul. It was bought by a Spanish Jew; but he's never lived in it and never let it."

"Well, then, where *did* she come from? Not out of the Fourth Dimension? Who *was* she? Not a wraith, an apparition? Why *will* you entertain such weird conjectures?"

"She must have come from Bayonne. An officer's wife, beyond a doubt."

"Oh, you're perfectly remorseless," sighed Paul, and changed the subject. But he was unconvinced. Officers' wives, in garrison towns like Bayonne, had, in his experience, always been, as he expressed it, frowsy and provincial.

IV

One would think, by this time, the priest, poor man, had earned a moment of mental rest; but Paul's thirst for knowledge was insatiable. He began to ply him with questions about the Queen. And though André could tell him very little, and though he had heard all that the night before from Manuela, it interested him curiously to hear it repeated.

It amounted to scarcely more than a single meagre fact. A few months after the divorce, she had returned to Granjolaye, and she had never once been known to set her foot beyond the limits of her garden from that day to this. She had arrived at night, attended by her two German ladies-in-waiting. A carriage had met her at the railway station in Bayonne, and set her down at the doors of her Château, where her aunt, old Mademoiselle Henriette, awaited her. What manner of life she led there, nobody had the poorest means of discovering. Her own servants (tongue-tied by fear or love) could not be got to speak; and from the eyes of all outsiders she was sedulously screened. Paul could imagine her, in her great humiliation, solitary among the ruins of her high destiny, hiding her wounds; too sensitive to face the curiosity, too proud to brook the pity, of the world. She seemed to him a very grandiose and tragic figure, and he lost himself musing of her — her with whom he had played at being married, when they were children here, so long, so long ago. She was the daughter, the only child and heiress, of the last Duc de la Granjolaye de Ravanches, — the same nobleman of whom it was told that when Louis Napoleon, meaning to be gracious, said to him, "You bear a great name, Monsieur," he had answered sweetly, "The greatest of all, I think." It is certain he was the head of one of the most illustrious houses in the noblesse of Europe, descended directly and legitimately, through the Bourbons, from Saint Louis of France; and, to boot, he was immensely rich, owning (it was said) half the iron mines in the north of Spain, as well as a great part of the city of Bayonne. Paul's grandmother, the Comtesse de Louvance, was his next neighbor. Paul remembered him vaguely as a tall, drab, mild-mannered man, with a receding chin, and a soft, rather piping voice, who used to tip him, and have him over a good deal to stay at Granjolaye.

On the death of Madame de Louvance, the property of Saint-Graal had passed to her son, Edmond, — André's feu Monsieur le Comte. Edmond rarely lived there, and never asked his sister or her boy there; whence, twenty years ago, at the respective ages of thirteen and eleven, Paul and Hélène had vanished from each other's ken. But Edmond never married, either; and when, last winter, he died, he left a will making Paul his heir. Of Hélène's later history Paul knew as much as all the world knows, and no more — so much, that is, as one could gather from newspapers and public rumor. He knew of her father's death, whereby she had become absolute mistress of his enormous fortune. He knew of her princely marriage, and of her elevation by the old king to her husband's rank of Royal Highness. He knew of that swift series of improbable deaths which had culminated in her husband's accession to the throne, and how she had been crowned Queen Consort. And then he knew that three or four years afterwards she had sued for and obtained a Bull of Separation from the Pope, on the plea of her husband's infidelity and cruelty. The infidelity, to be sure, was no more than, as a Royalty, if not as a woman, she might have bargained for and borne with; but everybody remembers the stories of the king's drunken violence that got bruited about at the time. Everybody will remember, too, how, the Papal Separation once pronounced, he had retaliated upon her with a decree of absolute divorce, and a sentence of perpetual banishment, voted by his own parliament. Whither she had betaken herself after these troubles Paul had never heard — until, yesterday, arriving at Saint-Graal, they told him she was living cloistered like a nun at Granjolaye.

News travels fast and penetrates everywhere in that lost corner of garrulous Gascony. The news that Paul had taken up his residence at Saint-Graal could scarcely fail to reach the Queen. Would she remember their childish intimacy? Would she make him a sign? Would she let him see her, for old sake's sake? Oh, in all probability, no. Most certainly, no. And yet — and yet he could n't forbid a little furtive hope to flicker in his heart.

V

It was only April, but the sun shone with midsummer strength.

After André left him, he went down into the garden.

From a little distance the house, against the sky, looked insubstantial, a water-color, painted in gray and amber on a field of luminous blue. If he had wished it, he could have bathed himself in flowers; hyacinths, crocuses, jonquils, camellias, roses, grew round him everywhere, sending up a symphony of warm odors; further on, in the grass, violets, anemones, celandine; further still, by the margins of the pond, narcissuses, and tall white flowers-de-luce; and, in the shrubberies, satiny azaleas; and overhead, the magnolia-trees, drooping with their freight of ivory cups. The glass doors of the orangery stood open, a cloud of sweetness hanging heavily before them. In the park, the chestnuts were in full leaf; and surely a thousand birds were twittering and piping amongst their branches.

"Oh, bother! How it cries out for a woman," said Paul. "It's such a waste of good material."

The beauty went to one's head. One craved a sympathetic companion to share it with, a woman on whom to lavish the ardors it enkindled. "If I don't look out I shall become sentimental," the lone man told himself. "Nature's so fearfully lacking in tact. Fancy her singing an epithalamium in a poor fellow's ears, when he does n't know a single human woman nearer than Paris." To make matters worse, the day ended in a fiery sunset, and then there was a full moon; and in the rosery a nightingale performed its sobbing serenade. "Please go out and give that bird a penny, and tell him to go away," Paul said to a servant. It was all very well to jest, but at every second breath he sighed profoundly. I'm afraid he *had* become sentimental. It seemed a serious pity that what his heart was full of should spend itself on the incapable air. His sense of humor was benumbed. And when, presently, the frogs in the pond, a hundred yards away, set up their monotonous plaintive concert, he laid down his arms. "It's no use, I'm in for it," he confessed. After all, he was out of England. He was in Gascony, the borderland between amorous France and old romantic Spain.

I don't know whom his imagination dwelt the more fondly with: the stricken Queen, beyond there, alone in the darkness and the silence, where the night lay on the forest of Granjolaye; or the pale horsewoman of the morning.

But surely, as yet, he had no ghost of a reason for dreaming that the two were one and the same.

VI

"Now, let's be logical," he said next morning. "Let's be logical and hopeful — yet not too hopeful, not utopian. Let's look the matter courageously in the face. Since she rode there once, why may she not ride again in the Sentier des Contrebandiers? Why may n't she ride there often — even daily? I think that's logical. Don't *you* think that's logical?"

The person he addressed, a tall, slender young man, with a fresh-colored skin, a straight nose, and rather a ribald eye, was vigorously brushing a head of yellowish hair in the looking-glass before him.

"Tush! But of course *you* think so," Paul went on. "You always think as I do. If you knew how I despise a sycophant! And yet — you're not bad looking. No, I'll be hanged if I can honestly say that you're bad looking. You've got nice hair, and plenty of it; and there's a weakness about your mouth and chin that goes to my heart. I hate firm people. — What? So do you? I thought so. — Ah, well, my poor friend, you're booked for a shocking long walk this morning. You must summon your utmost fortitude. — 'Under the greenwood tree, who loves to lie with me?'" he carolled forth, to Marzials's tune. "But come! I say! That's anticipating."

And he set forth for the Smugglers' Pathway, — where, sure enough, she rode again. As she passed him, her eyes met his: at which he was conscious of a good deal of interior commotion. "By Jove, she's magnificent, she's really stunning," he exclaimed to himself. He perceived that she was rather a big woman, tall, with finely rounded, smoothly flowing lines. Her hair, — velvety blue-black in its shadows, — where the light caught it was dully iridescent. Her features were irregular enough to give her face a high degree of individuality, yet by no means to deprive it of delicacy or attractiveness. She had a superb white throat, and a soft voluptuous chin; and "As I live, I never saw such a mouth," said Paul.

Where did she come from? Bayonne? Never. André might have been mistaken about Château

Yroulte; the Spanish Jew had perhaps sold it, or found a tenant. Or, further afield, there were Châteaux Labenne, Saumuse, d'Orthevielle. Or else, the Queen had a guest.

"Anyhow," he mused, when he got home, "that makes five, six miles that you have tramped to enjoy an instant's glimpse of her. Fortunately they say walking is good for the constitution. It only shows what extremities a country life may drive one to."

The next day, not only did her eyes meet his, but he could have sworn that she almost smiled. Oh, a very furtive smile, the mere transitory suggestion of a smile. But the inner commotion was more marked.

The next day (the fourth) she undoubtedly did smile, and slightly inclined her head. He removed his hat, and went home, and waited impatiently for twenty-four hours to wear away. "She smiled — she bowed," he kept repeating. But, alas! he couldn't forget that in that remote countryside it is very much the fashion for people who meet in the roads and lanes to bow as they pass.

On the fifth, sixth, seventh, and eighth days she bowed and smiled.

"I fairly wonder at myself — to walk that distance for a bow and smile," said Paul. "To-morrow I'm going to speak. Faut brusquer les choses."

And he penetrated into the forest, firmly determined to speak. "Only I can't seem to think of anything very pat to say," he sighed. "Hello! She's off her horse."

She was off her horse, standing beside it, holding the loose end of a strap in her hand.

Providence was favoring him. Here was his obvious chance. Something was wrong. He could offer his assistance. And yet, that inner commotion was so violent, he felt a little bewildered about the mot juste. He approached her gradually, trying to compose himself and collect his wits.

She looked up, and said in French, "I beg your pardon. Something has come undone. Can you help me?"

Her voice was delicious, cool and smooth as ivory. His heart pounded. He vaguely bowed, and murmured, "I should be delighted."

She stood aside a little, and he took her place. He bent over the strap that was loose, and bit his lips, and cursed his embarrassment. "Come, I must n't let her think me quite an ass." He was astonished at himself. That he should still be capable of so strenuous a sensation! "And I had thought I was blasé!" He was intensely conscious of the silence, of the solitude and dimness of the forest, and of their isolation there, so near to each other, that superb pale woman and himself. But his eyes were bent on the misbehaving strap, which he held helplessly between his fingers.

At last he looked up at her. "How warm and beautiful and fragrant she is," he thought. "With her white face, with her dark eyes, with those red lips and that splendid figure — what an heroic looking woman!"

"This is altogether disgraceful," he said, "and I assure you I'm covered with confusion. But I won't dissemble. I have n't the remotest notion what needs to be done. I'm afraid this is the first time in my life I have ever touched anything belonging to a horse."

He said it with a pathetic drawl, and she laughed: "And yet you're English."

"Oh, I dare say I'm English enough. Though I don't see how you knew it. Don't tell me you knew it from my accent."

"Oh, non pas," she hastened to protest. "But you're the new owner of Saint-Graal. Everybody of the country knows, of course, that the new owner of Saint-Graal, Mr. Warringwood, is English."

"Ah, then she's of the country," was Paul's mental note.

"And I thought all Englishmen were horsemen," she went on.

"Oh, there are a few bright exceptions — there's a little scattered remnant. It's the study of my life to avoid being typical."

"Ah, well, then give *me* the strap."

He gave her the strap, and in the twinkling of an eye she had snapped the necessary buckle. Then she looked up at him and smiled oddly. It occurred to him that the entire comedy of the strap had perhaps been invented as an excuse for opening a conversation; and he was at once flattered and disappointed.

"Oh, if she's that sort . . ." he thought.

"I'm heart-broken not to have been able to serve you," he said.

"You can help me to mount," she answered.

And, before he quite knew how it was done, he had helped her to mount, and she was galloping down the path. The firm grasp of her warm gloved hand on his shoulder accompanied him to Saint-

Graal. "It's amazing how she sticks in my mind," he said. He really couldn't fix his attention on any other subject. "I wonder who the deuce she is. She's giving me my money's worth in walking. That business of the strap was really brazen. Still, one mustn't quarrel with the means if one desires the end. I hope she *isn't* that sort."

VII

On the tenth, eleventh, and twelfth days she passed him with a bow and a good-morning.

"This is too much!" he groaned, in the silence of his chamber. "She's doing it with malice. I'll not be trifled with. I — I'll do something desperate. I'll pretend to faint, and she'll have to get down and bandage up my wounds."

On the thirteenth day, as they met, she stopped her horse.

"You're at least typically English in one respect," she said.

"Oh, unkind lady! To announce it to me in this sudden way. Then my life's a failure."

"I mean in your fondness for long walks."

"Ah, then, you're totally in error. I hate long walks."

"But it's a good ten kilometres to and from your house; and you do it every morning."

"That's only because there aren't any omnibuses or cabs or things. And" (he reminded himself that if she was that sort, he might be bold) "I'm irresistibly attracted here."

"It's very pretty," she admitted, and rode on.

He looked after her, grinding his teeth. *Was* she that sort? "One never can tell. Her face is so fine — so noble even."

The next day, "Yes, I suppose it's very pretty. But I wasn't thinking of Nature," he informed her, as she approached.

She drew up.

"Oh, it has its human interest too, no doubt." She glanced in the direction of the Château of Granjolaye.

"The Queen," said he. "But one never sees her."

"That adds the charm of mystery, don't you feel? To think of that poor young exiled woman, after so grand a beginning, ending so desolately, — shut up alone in her mysterious castle! It's like a legend."

"Then you're not of her Court?"

"I? Of her Court? Mais quelle idée!"

"It was only a hypothesis. Of course, you know I'm devoured by curiosity. My days are spent in wondering who you are."

She laughed. "You must have a care, or you'll be typical," she warned him.

"I never said I wasn't human," he called after her, as she cantered away.

VIII

The next day still (the fifteenth), "Haven't I heard you lived at Saint-Graal when you were a child?" she asked.

"If you have, for once in a way rumor has told the truth. I lived at Saint-Graal till I was thirteen."

"Then perhaps you knew her?"

"Her?"

"The Queen,—Mademoiselle de la Granjolaye de Ravanches."

"Oh, I knew her very well—when we were children."

"Tell me all about her."

"It would be a long story."

She leaped from her horse; then, raising her riding whip, and looking the animal severely in the eye, "Bézigue! Attention!" she said impressively. "You 're to stop exactly where you are, and not play any tricks. Entendu? Bien." She moved a few steps down the pathway, and stopped at an opening among the trees, where the ground was a cushion of bright green moss. "By Jove! she *is* at her ease," thought Paul, who followed her. "How splendidly she walks! what undulations!" From the French point of view, as she must be aware, the situation gave him all sorts of rights.

She sank softly, gracefully, upon the moss. "It's a long story. Tell it me," she commanded, and pointed to the earth. He sat down facing her, at a little distance.

"It's odd you should have chosen this place," said he.

"Odd? Why?" She looked at him inquiringly. For a moment their eyes held each other; and all at once the blood swept through him with suffocating violence. She was so beautiful, so sumptuous, so warmly and richly feminine; and surely the circumstances were not anodyne. Her softly rounded face, its very pallor, the curve and color of her lips, her luminous dark eyes, the smooth modulations of her voice, and then her loose abundance of black hair, and the swelling lines of her breast, the fluent contour of her waist and hips, under the fine black cloth of her dress, — all these, with the silence of the forest, the heat of the southern day, the woodland fragrances of which the air was full, and the sense of being intimately alone with her, set up within him a turbulent vibration, half of delight, half of pained suspense. And the complaisant informality with which she met him played a sustaining counterpoint. "What luck, what luck, what luck!" were the words which shaped themselves to the strong beating of his pulses. What would happen next? Whither would it lead? He had savored the bouquet, he was famished to taste the wine. And yet, so complicated are our human feelings, he was obscurely vexed. Only two kinds of woman, he would have maintained yesterday, could conceivably do a thing like this, — an ingénue, or "that sort." She wasn't an ingénue. Something, at the same time, half assured him that she wasn't "that sort," either. But — the circumstances! The situation!

"Why odd?" she repeated.

"Oh, I don't want to talk about the Queen," he said, in a smothered voice.

"The oddity relates itself to the Queen?"

"Oh, this is where we used to waste half our lives when we were children. That's all. This was our favorite nook."

"Perfect, then, for the story you're going to tell me."

"What story?"

"You said it was a long story."

"There's really no story at all." His eyes were fastened upon her hands, small and tapering in their tan gauntlets. The point of a patent-leather boot glanced from the edge of her skirt. A short gold watch-chain dangled from her breast, a cluster of charms at the end.

"You said it was a long story," she repeated sternly.

"It would be a dull one. We knew each other when we were infants, and used to play together. That is all."

"But what was she like? Describe her to me. I adore souvenirs d'enfance." Her eyes were bright with eagerness.

"Oh, she was very pretty; the prettiest little girl I've ever seen. She had the most wonderful eyes, — deep, deep, into which you could look a hundred miles; you know the sort, — dreamy, poetical, sad; oh! lovely eyes. And she used to wear her hair down her back; it was very long, and soft, — soft as smoke, almost; almost impalpable. She always dressed in white, — short white frocks, with broad sashes, red or blue. That was the fashion then for little girls. Perhaps it is still — I've never noticed."

"Yes. Don't stop. Go on."

"Dear me, I don't know what to say. I used to see her a good deal, because they were our neighbors. Her father used to ask me over to stay at Granjolaye. She needed a playmate, and I was the only one available. Sometimes she would come and spend a day at Saint-Graal. Do you know Granjolaye? The castle? It's worth going over. It used to belong to the Kings of Navarre, you know. We used to play together in the great audience chamber, and chase each other through the secret passages in the walls. At Saint-Graal we confined ourselves to the garden. Her head was full of the queerest romantic notions. You couldn't persuade her that the white irises that grew about our pond weren't enchanted princesses. One day we filled a bottle with holy water at the Church, and then she sprinkled them with it, pronouncing an incantation. 'If ye were born as ye are, remain as ye are; but if ye were born otherwise, resume your original shapes.' They remained as they were; but that didn't shake her faith. Something was amiss with the holy water, or with the form of her incantation."

She laughed softly. "Then she was nice? You liked her?" she asked.

"Oh, I was passionately in love with her. All children are passionately in love with somebody, aren't they? A real grande passion. It began when I was about ten." He broke off, to laugh. "Do you care for love stories? I'm a weary, way-worn man; but upon my word, I've never in all my life felt any such intense emotion for a woman, anything that so nearly deserved to be called *love*, as I felt for Hélène de la Granjolaye when I was an infant. Night after night I used to lie awake thinking how I loved her — longing to tell her so — planning how I would, next day — composing tremendous declarations — imagining her response — and waiting in a fever of impatience for the day to come. But then, when I met her, I didn't dare. Bless me, how

I used to thrill at sight of her, with love, with fear! How I used to look at her face, and pine to kiss her! If her hand touched mine, I almost fainted. It's very strange that children before their teens should be able to experience the whole gamut of the spiritual side of love; and yet it's certain."

She was looking at him with intent eyes, her lips parted a little. "But you did tell her at last, I hope?" she said anxiously.

He had got warmed to his subject, and her interest inspired him.

"Oh, at last! It was here — in this very spot. I had picked a lot of celandine, and stuck them about in her hair, where they shone like stars. Oh, the joy of being allowed to touch her hair! It made utterance a necessity. I fumbled and stammered, and blushed and thrilled, and almost choked. And at last I blurted it out. 'I love you so — I love you so.' That — after the eloquent declarations I had composed overnight!"

"And she?"

"She answered quite simply, 'Et moi, je t'aime tant, aussi.' And then she began to cry. And when I asked her what she was crying for, she explained that I oughtn't to have left her in doubt for so long; she had been so unhappy from fear that I didn't 'love her so.' She was quite unfemininely frank, you see. Oh, the ecstasy of that hour! The ecstasy of our first kiss! From that time on it was 'mon petit mari' and 'ma petite femme.' The greatest joy in life for me, for us, was to sit together, holding each other's hands, and repeating from time to time, 'J' t'aime tant, j' t'aime tant.' Now and then we would vary it with a fugue upon our names— 'Hélène!'—'Paul!'" He laughed. "Children, with their total lack of humor, are the drollest of created beings, aren't they?"

"Oh, I don't think it's droll. I know all children have those desperate love affairs; but they seem to me pathetic. How did it go on?"

"Oh, for two or three years we lived in Paradise. There were no other boys in the neighborhood, so she was constant."

"For three years? And then?"

"Then my grandmother died, and I was carried off to Paris. She remained here; and so it ended."

"And when did you meet her next? After you were grown up?"

"I have never met her since."

"You must have followed her career with a special interest, though?"

"Ah, quant à ça!"

"Her marriage, her coronation, her divorce. Poor Woman! What she must have suffered! Have you made any attempt to see her since you came back to Saint-Graal?"

"Ah, merci, non! If she wanted to see me, she'd send for me."

"She sees no one, everybody says. But I should think she'd like to see you—her old playmate. If she *should* send for you— But I suppose I mustn't ask you to tell me about it afterwards? Of course, like everybody else in her neighborhood, I'm awfully interested in her."

There was a moment's silence. She looked at the moss beneath her, and stroked it lightly with a finger-tip. Paul looked at her.

"You're horribly unkind," he said, at last.

"Unkind?" She raised wide eyes of innocent surprise.

"You know I'm in an agony of curiosity."

"About what?"

"About you."

"Me?"

"Yourself."

She lifted the cluster of charms at the end of her watch-chain. One of them was a tiny golden whistle. On this she blew, and Bézigue came trotting up. She mounted him to-day without Paul's assistance. Smiling down on the young man, she said, "Oh, after the reckless way in which I've cast the conventions to the winds, you really can't expect me to give you my name and address." And before he could answer, she was gone.

He walked about for the rest of the day in a great state of excitement. "My dear," he told himself, "if you're not careful, something serious will happen to you."

IX

When he woke up he saw that it was raining; and in that part of the world it really never does rain but it pours. Needless to touch upon the impatient ennui with which he roamed the house. He sent for André to lunch with him.

"André, can't you do something to stop this rain?" he asked; but André stared. "Oh, I was thinking of the priests of Baal," Paul explained. "I beg your pardon." And after the coffee, "Let's go up and play in the garret," he proposed; at which André stared harder still. "We always used to play in the garret on rainy days," Paul reminded him. "Mais, ma foi, monsieur, nous ne sommes plus des gosses," André answered.

"Is there any news about the Queen?" Paul asked.

"There's never any news from Granjolaye," said André.

"And the lady I met in the forest? Have you any new theory who she is?"

"An officer's wife from Ba——"

"André!" cried Paul. "If you say that again, I shall write to the Pope and ask him to disfrock you."

The next day was fine; but though he spent the entire morning in the Smuggler's Pathway, he did not meet her. "It's because the ground's still wet," he reasoned. "Oh, why don't things dry quicker?"

The next day he did meet her — and she passed him with a bow. He shook his fist at her unsuspecting back.

The next day he perceived Bézigue riderless near the opening among the trees. The horse neighed, as he drew near. She was seated on the moss. He stood still, and bowed tentatively from the path. "Are you disengaged? May I come in?" he asked.

"Oh, do," she answered. "And — won't you take a seat?"

"Thank you," and he placed himself beside her.

"Tell me about your life afterwards," she said.

"My life afterwards? After what?"

"After you were carried off to Paris."

"What earthly interest can *that* have?"

"I want to know."

"It was the average life of the average youth whose family is in average circumstances."

"You went to school?"

"What makes you doubt it? Do I seem so illiterate?"

"Where? In England? Eton? Harrow?"

"No, in Paris. The Lycée Louis le Grand. Oh, I have received an education — no expense was spared. I forget how many years I passed à faire mon droit in the Latin Quarter. You'd be surprised if you were to discover what a lot I know. Shall I prove to you that the sum of the angles of a right-angled triangle is equal to two right angles? Or conjugate the verb amo? Or give you a brief summary of the doctrines of Aristotle? Or an account of the life and works of Gustavus Adolphus?"

"When did you go to England?"

"Not till Necessity drove me there. I had to eke out a meagre patrimony. I went to England to seek my fortune."

"Did you find it?"

"I never had the knack of finding things. When my father used to send me into the library to fetch a book, or my mother into her dressing-room to fetch her scissors, I could never find them. I looked for it everywhere, but I couldn't find it."

"What did you do?"

"I lived by my wits. Chevalier d'industrie."

"Ah, non. Je ne crois pas."

"You don't believe my wits were sufficient to the task? I was like the London hospitals, — practically unendowed; only they wouldn't support me by voluntary contributions. So — I wrote for the newspapers, I 'm afraid."

"For the newspapers?"

"Oh, I admit, it's scandalous. But you may as well know the worst. A penny-a-liner! But I sha'n't do so any more, now that I have stepped into the shoes of my uncle. You 'll never catch me fatiguing myself with work, now that I 've got enough to live on!"

"Lazy!"

"Oh, I 'm everything that's reprehensible."

"And you never married?"

"I don't think so."

"Are n't you sure?"

"As sure as one can be of anything in this doubtful world."

"But why did n't you?"

"Pas si bête. Marriage is such a bore. I never met a woman I could bear the thought of passing all my life with."

"Conceited!"

"I dare say. If you like false modesty better, I 'll try to meet your wishes. What woman would have had a poor devil like me?"

"Still, marriage is, after all, very much in vogue."

"Yes, but it's mad. Either you must love the woman you marry, or you must n't love her. But if you marry a woman without loving her, I hope you 'll not deny you 're doing a very shocking thing. If, on the contrary, you do love her, raison de plus for not marrying her. Fancy marrying a woman you love; and then, day by day, watching the beautiful wild-flower of love fatten into a domestic cabbage! Is n't that a syllogism?"

"You have been in love, then?"

"Never."

"Never?"

"Oh, I've made a fool of myself occasionally, of course. But I've never been in love."

"Except with Hélène de la Granjolaye?"

"Oh, yes, I was in love with her — when I was ten."

"Till you were . . . ?"

"Till I was . . . ?"

"How long did it take you to get over it, I mean?"

"I don't know; it wore away gradually. The tooth of time."

"You're not at all in love with her any more?"

"After twenty years? And she a Queen? I hope I know my place."

"But if you were to meet her again?"

"I should probably suffer a horrible disillusion."

"But you have found, at any rate, that 'first love is best'?"

"First and last. The last shall be first," he said oracularly.

"Don't you smoke?" she asked.

"Oh, one by one you drag my vices from me. Let me own, en bloc, that I have them all."

"Then you may light a cigarette and give me one."

He gave her a cigarette, and held a match while she lit it. Then he lit one for himself. Her manner of smoking was leisurely, luxurious. She inhaled the smoke, and let it escape slowly in a slender spiral. He looked at her through the thin cloud, and his heart closed in a convulsion. "How big and soft and rich — how magnificent she is — like some great splendid flower, heavy with sweetness!" he thought. He had to breathe deep to overcome a feeling of suffocation; he was trembling in every nerve, and he wondered if she perceived it. He divined the smooth perfection of her body, through the supple cloth that moulded it; he noticed vaguely that the dress she wore to-day was blue, not black. He divined the warmth of her round white throat, the perfume of her skin. "And how those lips could kiss!" his imagination shouted wildly. Again, the silence, the solitude and dimness of the forest, their intimate seclusion there, the great trees, the sky, the bright green cushion of moss, the few detached sounds, — bird-notes, rustling leaves, snapping twigs, — by which the silence was intensified; again all these lent an acuteness to his sensations. Her dark eyes were smiling lustrously, languidly, at the smoke curling in the air before her, as if they saw a vision in it.

"You're adorable at moments," he said at last.

"At moments! Thank you." She laughed.

"Oh, you can't expect me to pretend that I find you adorable always. There are times when I could fall upon you and exterminate you."

"Why?"

"When you passed me yesterday with a nod."

"'T was your own fault. You did n't look amusing yesterday."

"When you baffle my perfectly innocent desire to know whom I have the honor of addressing."

"Shall I summon Bézigue?" she asked, touching her bunch of charms.

He acted his despair.

"Besides, what does it matter? I know who *you* are," she went on. "Let that console you."

"Did I say you were adorable? You're hateful."

"What's in a name? Nothing but the power to compromise. Would you have me compromise myself more than I've done already? A woman who makes a man's acquaintance without an introduction, and talks about love, and smokes cigarettes, with him!" She gave a little shudder. "How horrible it sounds when you state it baldly."

"One must never state things baldly. One must qualify. It's the difference between Truth and mere Fact. Truth is Fact qualified. You must add that the woman knew the man by common report to be of the highest possible respectability, and that she saw for herself he was (alas!) altogether harmless. And then you must explain that the affair took place in the country, in the spring; and that the cigarettes were the properest conceivable sort of cigarettes, having been rolled by hand in England."

"You wouldn't believe me if I said I had never done such a thing before? They all say that, don't they?"

"Yes, they all say that. But, oddly enough, I do believe you."

"Then you're not entirely lost to grace, not thoroughly a cynic."

"Oh, there are *some* good women."

"And some good men?"

"Possibly. I've never happened to meet one."

"The eye of the beholder!"

"If you like. But I don't know. There are such things, no doubt, as cynics by temperament; congenital cynics. Then, indeed, you may cry: The eye of the beholder. But others become cynics, are driven into cynicism, by sad experience. I started in life with the rosiest faith in my fellow-man. If I've lost it, it's because he's always behaved shabbily to me, soon or late; always taking some advantage. The struggle for existence! We're all beasts, who take part in it; we must be, or we're devoured. Women for the most part are out of it. Anyhow, plus je vois les hommes, plus j'aime les femmes."

"Are you a beast too?"

"Oh, yes. But I don't bite. I'm the kind of beast that runs away. I lie by the fire and purr, but at the first sign of trouble I jump for the open door. That's why the other fellows always got the better of me. They knew I was a coward, and profited by the knowledge. If my dear good uncle hadn't died, I don't know how I should have lived."

"I'm afraid you have 'lived' too much."

"That was uncalled for."

"Or else your looks belie you."

"My looks?"

"You're so dissipated-looking."

"Dissipated-looking? I? Horror!"

"You've got such a sophisticated eye, if that suits you better. You look blasé."

"You're a horrid, rude, uncomplimentary thing."

"Oh, if you're going to call names, I must summon my natural protector." She blew on her golden whistle, and up trotted the obedient Bézigue.

That evening Paul said to himself, "I vastly fear that something serious *has* happened to you. No, she's everything you like, but she *isn't* that sort."

He was depressed, dejected — the reaction, no doubt, from the excitement of her presence. "She's married, of course; and of course she's got a lover. And of course she'll never care a pin for the likes of me. And of course she sees what's the matter with me, and is laughing in her sleeve. And I had thought myself impervious. Oh, damn all women."

X

"Don't stop; ride on," he called out to her, next morning; "I sha'n't be amusing to-day. I'm frightfully low in my mind."

"Perhaps it will amuse me to study you in a new aspect," she said. "You can entertain me with the story of your griefs."

"Bare my wounds to make a lady smile? Oh, anything to oblige you."

She leapt lightly from Bézigue, and sank upon the moss.

"What is it all about?"

"Oh, not what you imagine," said he. "It's about my debts."

"I had hoped it was about your sins."

"*My* sins! I'm kept awake at night by the thought of *yours*."

"Your conscience is too sensitive. Mine are but peccadillos."

"You say that because you've no sense of moral proportion. Are cruelty and dissimulation peccadillos?"

"They may be even virtues. It all depends. Discipline and reserve!"

"I'll forgive you everything if you'll tell me your name."

"Oh, I have debts, as well as you."

"What have debts to do with the question?"

"I owe something to my reputation."

"If we're going to consider our reputations, what of mine?"

"Yours has preceded you into the country," she said, and drew from her pocket a small thin volume, bound in gray cloth, with a gilt design.

"Oh, heavens!" cried Paul. "This is how one's past finds one out."

"Oh, some of them aren't bad," she said. "Wait, I'll read you one."

"Then you know English?"

"A leetle. Bot the one I shall read is in Franch."

And then she read out, in an enchanting voice, one of his own French sonnets. "That isn't bad," she added. "Do you think it hopelessly bad?"

"It shows promise, perhaps — when *you* read it."

"It is strange, though, that it should have been written by a man who had never been in love."

"Imagination! Upon my word, I never had been. Besides, the idea is stolen. It's almost a literal translation from Rossetti. What with a little imagination and a little ingenuity, one can do wonderfully well on other people's experience."

"I don't believe you. You have been in love a hundred times."

"Never."

"Never? Not even with Hélène de la Granjolaye de Ravanches?"

"Oh, I don't count my infancy. Never with anybody else."

"It's very strange," she said. "Tell me some more about her."

"Oh, bother her."

"I suppose when they carried you off to Paris you had a tearful parting ? Did you kick and scream and say you would n't go ? "

"Why do you always make me talk about the Queen ? "

"She interests me. And when you talk about the Queen, I rather like you. It is nice to see that there *was* a time when you were capable of an emotion."

"You fancy I 'm incapable now ? "

"Tell me about your leave-taking, your farewells."

"Bother our farewells."

"They must have been heart-rending ? "

"Probably."

"Don't you remember ? "

"Oh, yes, I remember."

"Go on. Don't make me drag it from you by inches. Tell it to me in a pretty melodious narrative. Either that, or — " she touched her whistle.

"That's barefaced intimidation."

She raised the whistle to her lips.

"Stay, stay!" he cried, "I yield."

"I wait," she answered.

He bent his brows for an instant, then looked up smiling. "If it puts you to sleep, you 'll know whom to blame."

"Yes, yes, go on," she said impatiently.

"Dear me, there 's nothing worth telling. It was a few weeks after my grandmother's death. We were going to Paris the next day. Her father drove over, with her, to say good-bye. Whilst he was with my people in the drawing-room, she and I walked in the garden. — I say, this is going to become frightfully sentimental, you know. Sure you want it ? "

"Go on. Go on."

"Well, we walked in the garden; and she was crying, and I was beseeching her not to cry. She wore one of her white frocks, with a red sash, and her hair fell down her back below her waist. I was holding her hand. 'Don't cry, don't cry. I'll come back as soon as I'm a man, and marry you in real earnest!' I promised her." He paused and laughed.

"Go on. And she?"

"'Oh, aren't we married in real earnest now?' she asked. I explained that we weren't. 'You have to have the Notary over from Bayonne, and go to Church. I know, because that's how it was when my cousin Elodie was married. We're only married in play!' Then she asked if that wasn't just as good. 'Things one does in play are always so much nicer than real things,' she said."

"Out of the mouths of babes and sucklings! She had a prophetic soul."

"Hadn't she? I admitted that that was true. But I added that perhaps when people were grown-up and could do exactly as they pleased, it was different,—perhaps real things would come to be pleasant too."

"Have you found them so?"

"I suppose I can't be quite grown-up, for I've never yet had a chance to do exactly as I pleased."

"Poor young man. Go on."

"And, besides, I reminded her, all the married people we knew were really married, my father and mother, André's father and mother, my cousin Elodie. Hélène's mother was dead, so her parents did n't count. And I argued that we might be sure they found it fun to be really married, or else they would n't keep it up. 'Oh, well, then, I suppose we 'll have to be really married too,' she consented. 'But it seems as though it never could be as nice as this. If only you were n't going away!' Whereupon I promised again to come back, if she 'd promise to wait for me, and never love anybody else, and never, never, never allow another boy to kiss her. 'Oh, never, never, never,' she assured me. Then her father called her, and they drove away."

"And you went to Paris and forgot her. Why were you false to your engagement?"

"Oh, she had allowed another boy to kiss her. She had married a German prince. Besides, I received a good deal of discouragement from my family. The next day, in the train, I confided our understanding to my mother. My mother seemed to doubt whether her father would like me as a son-in-law. I was certain he would; he was awfully good-natured; he had given me two louis as a parting tip. 'But do you think he 'll care to let his daughter marry a bourgeois?' my mother asked. 'A what?' cried I. 'A bourgeois,' said my mother. 'I ain't a bourgeois,' I retorted indignantly. 'What are you then?' pursued my mother. I explained that my grandmother had been a countess, and my uncle was a count; so how could I be a bourgeois? 'But what is your father?' my mother asked. Oh, my father was 'only an Englishman.' But that did n't make me a bourgeois? 'Yes, it does,' my mother said. 'Just because my father's English?' 'Because he 's a commoner, because he is n't noble.' 'But then — then what did you go and marry him for?' I stammered. 'Where would you have been if I had n't?' my mother inquired. That puzzled me for a moment, but then I answered, 'Well, if you'd married a Frenchman, a Count or a Duke or something, I should n't have been a bourgeois;' and my mother confessed that that was true enough. 'I don't care if I *am* a bourgeois,' I said at last. 'When I'm big I'm going back to Saint-Graal; and if her father won't let me really marry her, because I'm a bourgeois, then we'll just go on making believe we're married.'"

She laughed. "And now you are big, and you've come back to Saint-Graal, and your lady-love is at Granjolaye. Why don't you call on her and offer to redeem your promise?"

"Why does n't she send for me — bid me to an audience?"

"Perhaps her prophetic soul warns her how you'd disappoint her."

"Do you think she'd be disappointed in me?"

"Are n't you disappointed in yourself?"

"Oh, dear, no; I think I'm very nice."

"*I* should be disappointed in myself, if I were a man who had been capable of such an innocent, sweet affection as yours for Hélène de la Granjolaye, and had then gone and soiled myself with the mud of what they call life." She spoke earnestly; her face was grave and sad.

He was surprised, and a little alarmed. "Do you mean by that that you think I'm a bad lot?" he asked.

"You said the other day — yesterday was it? — that you had made a fool of yourself on various occasions."

"Well?"

"Did the process not generally involve making a fool of a woman too?"

"Reciprocity? Perhaps."

"And what was it you always said to them?"

"Oh, I suppose I did."

"You told them you loved them?"

"I'm afraid so."

"And was it true?"

"No."

"Well, then!"

"Ah, but they weren't deceived; they never believed it. That's only a convention of the game, a necessary formula, like the 'Dear' at the beginning of a letter."

"You have 'lived;' you have 'lived.' You'd have been so unique, so rare, so much more interesting, if instead of going and 'living' like other men, you had remained true to the ideal passion of your childhood."

"I had the misfortune to be born into the world, and not into a fairy tale, you see. But it's a perfectly gratuitous assumption that I have 'lived.'"

"Can you honestly tell me you haven't?" she asked, very soberly, with something like eagerness; her pale face intent.

"As a matter of fact . . . Oh, the worst of it is . . . I can't honestly say that I've never . . . But then, what do you want to rake up such matters for? It's not my fault if I've accepted the traditions of my century. Well, anyhow, you see I can't lie to you."

"You appear to find it difficult," she assented, rising.

"Well, what do you infer from that?"

She blew her whistle. "That — that you're out of training," she said lightly, as she mounted her horse.

"Oh," he groaned, "you're ——"

"What?"

"You beggar language."

She laughed and rode away.

"There, I've spoiled everything," Paul said, and went home, and passed a sleepless night.

XI

"I'll bet you sixpence she won't turn up to-day," he said to his friend in the glass, next morning; nevertheless he went into the forest, and there she was. But she did not offer to dismount.

"Isn't there another inference to be drawn from my inability to lie to you?" he asked.

She smiled on him from her saddle. "Oh, perhaps there are a hundred."

"Don't you think a reasonable inference is that — I love you?"

She laughed.

"You know I love you," he persisted.

"Oh, the conventions of the game! the necessary formula, like 'Dear' at the beginning of a letter!" she cried.

"You don't believe me?"

"Qui m'aime me suive," she said, spurring Bézigue into a rapid trot.

XII

But the next day he found her already installed in their nook among the trees.

"I hate people who doubt my word," he said.

"Oh, now you hate me?"

"I love you. I love you."

She drew away a little.

"Oh, you need n't be afraid. I sha'n't touch you. Why won't you believe me?"

"Do men always glare savagely like that at women they love?"

"Why won't you believe me?"

"How long have you known me?"

"All my life. A fortnight — three weeks. But that's a lifetime."

"And what do you know about me?"

"Everything. I know that you're adorable. And I adore you."

"Adorable — at moments. Do you know whether I am — married, for example?"

"I know that if you are, I should like to kill your husband. Are you? Tell me. Put me out of suspense. Let me go home and open a vein."

"Have I the air of a jeune fille?"

"Thank goodness, no. But there are such things as widows."

"And what more do you know about me?"

"Tell me — *are* you married?"

"You may suppose that I'm a widow."

"Thank God!"

She laughed.

"Will you marry me?" he asked.

"Oh, marriage is such a bore," she reminded him.

"Will you marry me?"

"No," she said. "But you may give me a cigarette."

And for a while they smoked without speaking.

"I hope at any rate you believe me now," he said.

"Because you've offered to make the crowning sacrifice? By the by, what is my number?"

"Oh, don't," he cried. "You're the only woman I've ever cared a straw for; and I care so much for you that I'd — I'd —" He stammered, seeking for a thing to say he'd do.

"You'd go to the length of marrying me. Only fancy!"

"Oh, you may laugh. But I love you."

"Do you love me as much as you used to love Hélène?"

"I love you as much as it's possible for a man to love a woman."

"Do you know what I think?"

"No. What?"

"If she were to send for you, one of these days, I think you'd forget me utterly. Your old love would come back at sight of her. They say she's very good-looking."

"Nonsense."

"I should like to try you."

"I shouldn't fear the trial."

"Il ne faut jamais dire à la fontaine, je ne boirai pas de ton eau."

"But when one's thirst is for wine?"

"It shows that there's some relation between psychology and geography, after all," she said.

"What do you mean?"

"Oh, the influence of places. It is here that you and she used to play a fugue on each other's names. The spot raises ghosts. Ghosts of your old emotions. And I'm conveniently at hand."

"If you could see yourself, you'd understand that the influence of places is superfluous. If you could look into my heart you'd recognize that my emotion is scarcely a ghost."

"There's one thing I *should* like to see," she said. "I should very much like to look into your garden at Saint-Graal."

"Would you?" he cried eagerly. "When will you come?"

"Whenever you like."

"Now. At once."

"No. To-morrow."

"To-morrow morning?"

"Yes. You can await me at your park-gates at eleven."

"Then you'll lunch with me?"

"No. . . . Perhaps."

"You're an angel!"

And he trudged home on the air. "If a woman will listen!" his heart sang. "If a woman will come to see your garden!"

XIII.

That evening a servant handed him a letter.

"A footman has brought it from Granjolaye, and is waiting for an answer."

The letter ran thus: —

"Monsieur: — I am directed by Her Majesty the Queen Hélène to request the pleasure of your company at the Château de Granjolaye to-morrow at eleven. Her Majesty desires me to add that she has only to-day learned of your presence in the country.

"Agréez, Monsieur, l'assurance de mes sentiments distingués,

"Ctsse. de Wolfenbach."

"Oh, this is staggering," cried Paul. "What to do?" He walked backwards and forwards, pondering his reply. "I believe the only excuse that will pass with Royalty is illness or death. Shall I send word that I died suddenly this morning. Ah, well, here goes for a thumping lie."

And he wrote: —

"Madame, — I am unspeakably honored by Her Majesty's command, and in despair that the state of my health makes it impossible for me to obey it. I am confined to my bed by a severe attack of bronchitis. Pray express to Her Majesty my most respectful thanks as well as my profound regret. I shall hope to be able to leave my room at the week's end, when, if Her Majesty can be prevailed upon again to accord me an audience, I shall be infinitely grateful."

"There!" he muttered. "I have perjured my soul for you, and made myself appear ridiculous into the bargain. *Bronchitis!* But — à demain! Good — good Lord! if she shouldn't come?"

XIV

She came, followed by a groom. She greeted Paul with a smile that made his heart leap with a wild hope. Her groom led Bézigue away to the stables.

"Thank you," said Paul.

"For what?"

"For everything. For coming. For that smile."

"Oh."

They walked about the garden. "It is lovely. The prettiest garden of the neighborhood," she said. "Show me where the irises grow, by the pond." And when they had arrived there, "They do look like princesses, don't they? Your little friend had some perceptions. Show me where you and she used to sit down. I am tired."

He led her into a corner of the rosery. She sank upon the turf.

"It is nice here," she said, "and quite shut in. One would never know there was a house so near."

She had taken off one of her gloves. Her soft white hand lay languidly in her lap. Suddenly Paul seized it, and kissed it — furiously — again and again. She yielded it. It was sweet to smell, and warm. "My God, how I love you, how I love you!" he murmured.

When he looked up she was smiling. "Oh, you are radiant! You are divine!" he cried. And then her eyes filled with tears. "What is it? What is it? You are unhappy?"

"Oh, no," she said. "But to think — to think that after all these years of misery, of heartbreak, it should end like this, here."

"Here?" he questioned.

"I am glad your bronchitis is better, but you *can* invent the most awful fibs," she said.

He looked at her, while the universe whirled round him.

"Hélène!"
"Paul!"

XV

Her divorce did n't carry with it the right to marry again. But she said, "We can go on making believe we 're married. Things one does in play are always so much nicer than real things." And when he spoke of the "world," she answered, "I have nothing to fear or to hope from the world. It has done its worst by me already."

As they walked back to the house for luncheon, Paul looked into her face, and said, "I can't believe my eyes, you know."

She smiled and took his arm. "J' t'aime tant," she whispered.

"And now I can't believe my ears!"

And this would appear to be the end, but I suppose it can't be, for everybody says nowadays that nothing ever ends happily here below.

THE END.

THE KEYNOTES SERIES.

16mo, cloth. Each volume with a Title-page and Cover Design

By AUBREY BEARDSLEY.

Price, $1.00.

I. **KEYNOTES.** By GEORGE EGERTON.

II. **THE DANCING FAUN.** By FLORENCE FARR.

III. **POOR FOLK.** By FEDOR DOSTOIEVSKY. Translated from the Russian by LENA MILMAN. With an Introduction by GEORGE MOORE.

IV. **A CHILD OF THE AGE.** By FRANCIS ADAMS.

V. **THE GREAT GOD PAN AND THE INMOST LIGHT.** By ARTHUR MACHEN.

VI. **DISCORDS.** By GEORGE EGERTON.

VII. **PRINCE ZALESKI.** By M. P. SHIEL.

VIII. **THE WOMAN WHO DID.** By GRANT ALLEN.

IX. **WOMEN'S TRAGEDIES.** By H. D. LOWRY.

X. **GREY ROSES AND OTHER STORIES.** By HENRY HARLAND. *[In preparation.*

XI. **AT THE FIRST CORNER AND OTHER STORIES.** By H. B. MARRIOTT WATSON.

XII. **MONOCHROMES.** By ELLA D'ARCY. *[In preparation.*

XIII. **AT THE RELTON ARMS.** By EVELYN SHARP. *[In preparation.*

XIV. **THE GIRL FROM THE FARM.** By GERTRUDE DIX. *[In preparation.*

XV. **THE MIRROR OF MUSIC.** By STANLEY V. MAKOWER. *[In preparation.*

Sold by all Booksellers. Mailed, postpaid, on receipt of price, by the Publishers,

ROBERTS BROTHERS, BOSTON, MASS.

John Lane, The Bodley Head, Vigo Street, London, W.

Messrs. Roberts Brothers' Publications.

THE GREAT GOD PAN AND THE INMOST LIGHT.

BY ARTHUR MACHEN.

KEYNOTES SERIES.

16mo. Cloth. Price, $1.00.

A couple of tales by Arthur Machen, presumably an Englishman, published æsthetically in this country by Roberts Brothers. They are horror stories, the horror being of the vague psychologic kind and dependent, in each case, upon a man of science who tries to effect a change in individual personality by an operation upon the brain cells. The implied lesson is that it is dangerous and unwise to seek to probe the mystery separating mind and matter. These sketches are extremely strong and we guarantee the "shivers" to anyone who reads them. — *Hartford Courant.*

For two stories of the most marvelous and improbable character, yet told with wonderful realism and naturalness, the palm for this time will have to be awarded to Arthur Machen, for "The Great God Pan and the Inmost Light," two stories just published in one book. They are fitting companions to the famous stories by Edgar Allan Poe both in matter and style. "The Great God Pan" is founded upon an experiment made upon a girl by which she was enabled for a moment to see the god Pan, but with most disastrous results, the most wonderful of which is revealed at the end of the story, and which solution the reader will eagerly seek to reach. From the first mystery or tragedy follow in rapid succession. "The Inmost Light" is equally as remarkable for its imaginative power and perfect air of probability. Anything in the legitimate line of psychology utterly pales before these stories of such plausibility. *Boston Home Journal.*

Precisely who the great god Pan of Mr. Machen's first tale is, we did not quite discover when we read it, or, discovering, we have forgotten; but our impression is that under the idea of that primitive great deity he impersonated, or meant to impersonate, the evil influences that attach to woman, the fatality of feminine beauty, which, like the countenance of the great god Pan, is deadly to all who behold it. His heroine is a beautiful woman, who ruins the souls and bodies of those over whom she casts her spells, being as good as a Suicide Club, if we may say so, to those who love her; and to whom she is Death. Something like this, if not this exactly, is, we take it, the interpretation of Mr. Machen's uncanny parable, which is too obscure to justify itself as an imaginative creation and too morbid to be the production of a healthy mind. The kind of writing which it illustrates is a bad one, and this is one of the worst of the kind. It is not terrible, but horrible. — *R. H. S. in Mail and Express.*

Sold by all Booksellers. Mailed by Publishers,

ROBERTS BROTHERS, BOSTON, MASS.

Messrs. Roberts Brothers' Publications.

DISCORDS.

A Volume of Stories.

By GEORGE EGERTON, author of "Keynotes."

AMERICAN COPYRIGHT EDITION.

16mo. Cloth. Price, $1.00.

George Egerton's new volume entitled "Discords," a collection of short stories, is more talked about, just now, than any other fiction of the day. The collection is really stories for story-writers. They are precisely the quality which literary folk will wrangle over. Harold Frederic cables from London to the "New York Times" that the book is making a profound impression there. It is published on both sides, the Roberts House bringing it out in Boston. George Egerton, like George Eliot and George Sand, is a woman's *nom de plume*. The extraordinary frankness with which life in general is discussed in these stories not unnaturally arrests attention. — *Lilian Whiting.*

The English woman, known as yet only by the name of George Egerton, who made something of a stir in the world by a volume of strong stories called "Keynotes," has brought out a new book under the rather uncomfortable title of "Discords." These stories show us pessimism run wild; the gloomy things that can happen to a human being are so dwelt upon as to leave the impression that in the author's own world there is no light. The relations of the sexes are treated of in bitter irony, which develops into actual horror as the pages pass. But in all this there is a rugged grandeur of style, a keen analysis of motive, and a deepness of pathos that stamp George Egerton as one of the greatest women writers of the day. "Discords" has been called a volume of stories; it is a misnomer, for the book contains merely varying episodes in lives of men and women, with no plot, no beginning nor ending. — *Boston Traveller.*

This is a new volume of psychological stories from the pen and brains of George Egerton, the author of "Keynotes." Evidently the titles of the author's books are selected according to musical principles. The first story in the book is "A Psychological Moment at Three Periods." It is all strength rather than sentiment. The story of the child, of the girl, and of the woman is told, and told by one to whom the mysteries of the life of each are familiarly known. In their very truth, as the writer has so subtly analyzed her triple characters, they sadden one to think that such things must be; yet as they are real, they are bound to be disclosed by somebody and in due time. The author betrays remarkable penetrative skill and perception, and dissects the human heart with a power from whose demonstration the sensitive nature may instinctively shrink even while fascinated with the narration and hypnotized by the treatment exhibited. — *Courier.*

Sold by all Booksellers. Mailed by Publishers,

ROBERTS BROTHERS, BOSTON, MASS.

Messrs. Roberts Brothers' Publications.

THE WOMAN WHO DID.

BY GRANT ALLEN.

Keynotes Series. American Copyright Edition.

16mo. Cloth. Price, $1.00.

A very remarkable story, which in a coarser hand than its refined and gifted author could never have been effectively told; for such a hand could not have sustained the purity of motive, nor have portrayed the noble, irreproachable character of Herminia Barton. — *Boston Home Journal.*

"The Woman Who Did" is a remarkable and powerful story. It increases our respect for Mr. Allen's ability, nor do we feel inclined to join in throwing stones at him as a perverter of our morals and our social institutions. However widely we may differ from Mr. Allen's views on many important questions, we are bound to recognize his sincerity, and to respect him accordingly. It is powerful and painful, but it is not convincing. Herminia Barton is a woman whose nobleness both of mind and of life we willingly concede; but as she is presented to us by Mr. Allen, there is unmistakably a flaw in her intellect. This in itself does not detract from the reality of the picture. — *The Speaker.*

In the work itself, every page, and in fact every line, contains outbursts of intellectual passion that places this author among the giants of the nineteenth century. — *American Newsman.*

Interesting, and at times intense and powerful. — *Buffalo Commercial.*

No one can doubt the sincerity of the author. — *Woman's Journal.*

The story is a strong one, very strong, and teaches a lesson that no one has a right to step aside from the moral path laid out by religion, the law, and society. — *Boston Times.*

Sold by all Booksellers. Mailed, postpaid, on receipt of price, by the Publishers,

ROBERTS BROTHERS, BOSTON, MASS.

www.ingramcontent.com/pod-product-compliance
Lightning Source LLC
Chambersburg PA
CBHW020832230426
43666CB00007B/1198